MOTIVI
POCKE

THIRTY-FIRST EDITION

SPRING 1993

The Complete Guide to all BR-operated Locomotives

Peter Fox and
Richard Bolsover

PLATFORM
5

ISBN 1 872524 51 6

© 1993. Platform 5 Publishing Ltd., Wyvern House, Old Forge Business Park, Sark Road, Sheffield, S2 4HG.

CONTENTS

Livery Codes. . . . . Inside front cover
From the Publisher. 2
Notes 3
General Information on British Railways' Locomotives. 4
BR Diesel Locomotives. 7
BR Electric Locomotives. 53
BR Departmental Locomotives. 63
Eurotunnel Locomotives. 65
BR Locomotives Awaiting Disposal 67
Pool Codes & Allocations 79
Depot Codes. . . . . Inside back cover
Livery Codes . . . . Inside front cover

FROM THE PUBLISHER

Platform 5 Publishing are still the only company to provide the enthusiast or transport official with complete information on BR rolling stock. This book is updated to 4th June 1993 and is, at the time of publication, the most up-to-date publication of its type on the market.

This book also contains details of the stock of Eurotunnel.

In the centre of this issue will be found details of our book club which features pre-publication discounts on most Platform 5 books (excluding our BR pocket books). It is hoped that enthusiasts will find this facility convenient and cost effective.

We hope you like our modified page style. In addition to altering the page style, we have made one other change this issue. This concerns sub-classes 31/4, 31/5, 86/4 and 86/6, where the third digit changes too and fro, but the last two digits are in sequence. These are now listed in order of the last two digits.

NOTES

The following notes are applicable to locomotives:

LOCOMOTIVE CLASS DETAILS

Principal details and dimensions are given for each class in metric units. Imperial equivalents are also given for power. Maximum speeds are still quoted in miles per hour since the operating department of BR still uses imperial units. Since the present maximum permissible speed of certain classes of locomotives is different from the design speed, these are now shown separately in class details. In some cases certain low speed limits are arbitrary and may occasionally be raised raised when necessary if a locomotive has to be pressed into passenger service.

Standard abbreviations used are:

ABB	ABB Transportation Ltd.	kV	kilovolts
BR	British Railways	kW	kilowatts
BREL	British Rail Engineering Ltd.	lbf	pounds force
	(later BREL Ltd.)	mph	miles per hour
hp	horse power	RA	Route availability
kN	kilonewtons	t	tonnes

LOCOMOTIVE DETAIL DIFFERENCES

Detail differences which affect the areas and types of train which locos work are shown. Where detail differences occur within a class or part class of locos., these are shown against the individual loco number. Except where shown, diesel locomotives have no train heating equipment. Electric or electro-diesel locomotives are assumed to have train heating unless shown otherwise. Standard abbreviations used are:

a	Train air brakes only
c	Cab to shore radio-telephone fitted.
e	Fitted with electric heating apparatus (ETH).
r	Fitted with radio electronic token block equipment.
s	Slow speed control fitted (and operable).
t	Fitted with automatic vehicle identification transponders.
v	Train vacuum brakes only.
x	Dual train brakes (air & vacuum).
y	ETH equipped but equipment isolated.
+	Extended range locos with Additional fuel tank capacity compared with others in class.

NAMES AND ALLOCATIONS

All official names are shown as they appear on the locomotive i.e. all upper case or upper & lower case lettering.

(S) denotes stored serviceable and (U) stored unserviceable. Last known allocations of stored locomotives are shown, but readers should note that locomotives may not necessarily be stored at their home depots.

After the locomotive number are shown any notes regarding braking, heating etc., the livery code (in bold type), the pool code, the depot code and name if any. Locomotives which have been renumbered in recent years show the last number in parentheses after the current number. Where only a few locomotives in a class are named, these are shown in a separate table at the end of the class or sub-class.

Thus the layout is as follows:

No.	Old No.	Notes	Liv.	Pool	Depot	Name
47636	(47243)	+	**RX**	PXLB	CD	Restored

GENERAL INFORMATION ON BRITISH RAILWAYS' LOCOMOTIVES

CLASSIFICATION & NUMBERING

Initially BR diesel locomotives were allocated numbers in the 1xxxx series, with electrics allotted numbers in the 2xxxx series. Around 1957 diesel locomotives were allocated new four digit numbers with 'D' prefixes. Diesel electric shunters in the 13xxx series had the '1' replaced by a 'D', but diesel mechanical shunters were completely renumbered. Electric locomotives retained their previous numbers but with an 'E' prefix. When all standard gauge steam locomotives had been withdrawn, the prefix letter was removed.

In 1972, the present TOPS numbering system was introduced whereby the loco number consisted of a two-digit class number followed by a serial number. In some cases the last two digits of the former number were generally retained (classes 20, 37, 50), but in other classes this is not the case. In this book former TOPS numbers carried by converted locos. are shown in parentheses. Full renumbering information is to be found in the 'Diesel & Electric loco Register'. This is at present out of print, but a new edition may be published in the future.

Diesel locomotives are classified as "types" depending on their engine horsepower as follows:

Type	Engine hp.	Old Number Range	Current Classes
1	800 – 1000	D 8000 – D 8999	20
2	1001 – 1499	D 5000 – D 6499/D 7500 – D 7999	26, 31.
3	1500 – 1999	D 6500 – D 7499	33, 37.
4	2000 – 2999	D 1 – D 1999	47, 50.
5	3000 +	D 9000 – D 9499	56, 58, 59, 60.
Shunter	Under 300	D 2000 – D 2999	03.
Shunter	300 – 799	D 3000 – D 4999	08, 09.

Class 14 (650 hp diesel hydraulics) were numbered in the D95xx series.

Electric and electro-diesel locomotives are classified according their supply system. Locomotives operating on a d.c. system are allocated classes 71 – 80, whilst a.c. or dual voltage locomotives start at Class starting at 81. Departmental locomotives which remain self propelled or which are likely to move around on a day to day basis are classified 97.

WHEEL ARRANGEMENT

For main line diesel and electric locomotives the system whereby the number of driven axles on a bogie or frame is denoted by a letter (A = 1, B = 2, C = 3 etc.) and the number of undriven axles is noted by a number is used. The letter 'o' after a letter indicates that each axle is individually powered and a + sign indicates that the bogies are intercoupled.

For shunters and steam locomotives the Whyte notation is used. The number of leading wheels are given, followed by the number of driving wheels and then the trailing wheels. Suffix 'T' on a steam locomotive indicates a tank locomotive, and 'PT' a pannier tank loco.

HAULING CAPABILITY OF DIESEL LOCOS

The hauling capability of a diesel locomotive depends basically upon three factors:

1. Its adhesive weight. The greater the weight on its driving wheels, the greater the adhesion and thus more tractive power can be applied before wheel slip occurs.

2. The characteristics of its transmission. In order to start a train the locomotive has to exert a pull at standstill. A direct drive diesel engine cannot do this, hence the need for transmission. This may be mechanical, hydraulic or electric. The current BR standard for locomotives is electric transmission. Here the diesel engine drives a generator or alternator and the current produced is fed to the traction motors. The force produced by each driven wheel depends on the current in its traction motor. In other words the larger the current, the harder it pulls.

As the locomotive speed increases, the current in the traction motors falls hence the *Maximum Tractive Effort* is the maximum force at its wheels that the locomotive can exert at a standstill. The electrical equipment cannot take such high currrents for long without overheating. Hence the *Continuous Tractive Effort* is quoted which represents the current which the equipment can take continuously.

3. The power of its engine. Not all of this power reaches the rail as electrical machines are approximately 90% efficient. As the electrical energy passes through two such machines (the generator/alternator and the traction motors), the *Power At Rail* is about 81% (90% of 90%) of the engine power, less a further amount used for auxiliary equipment such as radiator fans, traction motor cooling fans, air compressors, battery charging, cab heating, ETH, etc. The power of the locomotive is proportional to the tractive effort times the speed. Hence when on full power there is a speed corresponding to the continuous tractive effort.

HAULING CAPABILITY OF ELECTRIC LOCOS

Unlike a diesel locomotive, an electric locomotive does not develop its power on board and its performance is determined only by two factors, namely its weight and the characteristics of its electrical equipment. Whereas a diesel locomotive tends to be a constant power machine, the power of an electric locomotive varies considerably. Up to a certain speed it can produce virtually a constant tractive effort. Hence power rises with speed according to the formula given in section 3 above, until a maximum speed is reached at which tractive effort falls, such that the power also falls. Hence the power at the speed corresponding to the maximum tractive effort is lower than the maximum.

BRAKE FORCE

The brake force is a measure of the braking power of a locomotive. This is shown on the locomotive data panels so that railway staff can ensure that sufficient brake power is available on freight trains.

TRAIN HEATING EQUIPMENT

Electric train heating (ETH) is now the standard system in use on BR for loco-hauled trains. Locomotives which were equipped to provide steam heating have had this equipment removed or rendered inoperable (isolated). Electric heat is provided from the locomotive by means of a separate alternator on the loco., except in the case of and classes 33 and 50 which have a d.c. generator. The *ETH Index* is a measure of the electrical power available for train heating. All electrically heated coaches have an ETH index and the total of these in a train must not exceed the ETH power of a locomotive.

ROUTE AVAILABILITY

This is a measure of a railway vehicle's axle load. The higher the axle load of a vehicle, the higher the RA number on a scale 1 to 10. Each route on BR has an RA number and in theory no vehicle with a higher RA number may travel on that route without special clearance. Exceptions are made, however.

MULTIPLE AND PUSH-PULL WORKING

Multiple working between diesel locomotives on BR has usually been provided by means of an electro-pneumatic system, with special jumper cables connecting the locos. A coloured symbol is painted on the end of the locomotive to denote which system is in use. Class 47/7 used a time-division multiplex (t.d.m.) system which utilised the existing RCH (an abbreviation for the former railway clearing house, a pre-nationalisation standards organisation) jumper cables for push-pull working. These had in the past only been used for train lighting control, and more recently for public address (pa) and driver – guard communication. A new standard t.d.m. system is now fitted to all a.c. electric locomotives and other vehicles, enabling them to work in both push-pull and multiple working modes.

BR DIESEL LOCOMOTIVES

CLASS 03   BR SHUNTER   0-6-0

Built: 1960 at BR Doncaster Works.
Engine: Gardner 8L3 of 152 kW (204 hp) at 1200 rpm.
Transmission: Mechanical. Fluidrive type 23 hydraulic coupling to Wilson-Drewry CA5R7 gearbox with SCG type RF11 final drive.
Max. Tractive Effort: 68 kN (15300 lbf).

Brake Force: 13 t.	**Length over Buffers:** 7.92 m.
Weight: 31 t.	**Wheel Diameter:** 1092 mm.
Max. Speed: 28 mph.	**RA:** 1.

Formerly numbered 2079.

03079 v   NKJD   RY |

CLASS 08   BR SHUNTER   0-6-0

Built: 1953 – 62 by BR at Crewe, Darlington, Derby, Doncaster or Horwich Works.
Engine: English Electric 6KT of 298 kW (400 hp) at 680 rpm.
Main Generator: English Electric 801.
Traction Motors: Two English Electric 506.
Max. Tractive Effort: 156 kN (35000 lbf).
Cont. Tractive Effort: 49 kN (11100 lbf) at 8.8 mph.

Power At Rail: 194 kW (260 hp).	**Length over Buffers:** 8.92 m.
Brake Force: 19 t.	**Wheel Diameter:** 1372 mm.
Design Speed: 20 mph.	**Weight:** 50 t.
Max. Speed: 15 or 20* mph.	**RA:** 5.

Non standard liveries:

08500 is red lined out in black & white.
08601 is London Midland & Scottish Railway black.
08642 is London & South Western Railway black and also carries its former number D 3809.
08721 is blue with a red & yellow stripe ("Red Star" livery).
08730/867 are BR black.
08793 is London & North Eastern Railway apple green.
08883 is Caledonian blue.
08907 is London & North Western Railway black.
08933 is as 'D' but with two orange cabside stripes.
08938 is grey and red.

n – Waterproofed for working at Oxley Carriage Depot.
z – Fitted with buckeye adaptor at nose end for HST depot shunting.
§ – Fitted with yellow flashing light and siren for working between Ipswich Yard and Cliff Quay.

Formerly numbered in series 3000 – 4192. 08600 was numbered 97800 whilst in departmental use between 1979 and 1989.

CLASS 08/0. Standard Design.

08388	a	F	FSNI	IM	08521	a		MSNA	AN
08389	a		FSNL	NL	08523	x		MSSR	RG
08393	a	D	MSSS	SF	08525	x	F	FSCK	KY
08397	a	F	MSNA	AN	08526	x		MSSS	SF
08401	a	D	FSNI	IM	08527	x	D	MSSS	SF
08402	a	D	MSNA	AN	08528	x	D	MSSM	MR
08405	a	D	FSNI	IM	08529	x		MSSM	MR
08410	a	D	MSSA	BR	08530	x	D	MSSS	SF
08411	a		FSNY	TE	08531	x	F	MSSS	SF
08413	a	D	MSCH	SF	08534	x	D	MSNU	CL
08414	a*§		MSSS	SF	08535	x	D	MSNB	BS
08415	x		MSNA	AN	08536	x		MSNE	DY
08417	a	D	MSCH	SF	08538	x	D	MSSM	MR
08418	a	F	FSCD	DR	08540	x	D	MSSM	MR
08428	a		MSNB	BS	08541	x	D	MSSS	SF
08441	a		FSCN	TO	08542	x	F	MSSS	SF
08442	a	F	FSCD	DR	08543	x	D	MSNB	BS
08445	a		FSNI	IM	08561	x		FSSA	AY
08447	a		MSNU	CL	08562	x		MSCH	DR
08448	a		MSNB	BS	08565	x		FSSM	ML
08449	a		FSCN	TO	08567	x		MSSB	BY
08451	x		MSSW	WN	08568	x		FSSM	ML
08454	x		MSSW	WN	08569	x		MSNA	AN
08460	a	F	MSSO	OC	08571	xz		FSSM	ML
08466	a	F0	FSNI	IM	08573	x		MSSS	SF
08472	a		MSCH	CD	08575	x	BS	FSNL	NL
08480	az		MSSO	OC	08576	x		MSSL	LA
08481	x		FSWK	CF	08577	x		FSNH	HT
08482	a	D	MSNA	AN	08578	x	R	FSNH	HT
08483	a	D	MSSA	BR	08580	x		MSSM	MR
08484	a	F	MSSB	BY	08581	x		FSNL	NL
08485	a		MSNA	AN	08582	a	D	FSNY	TE
08489	a	F	MSNA	AN	08583	x		FSCK	KY
08492	a		FSCN	TO	08585	x		MSNC	CD
08493	a		FSWK	CF	08586	a	F	FSSA	AY
08495	x		MSSM	MR	08587	x		FSNH	HT
08498	a		MSCH	SF	08588	xz	BS	FSNL	NL
08499	a	F	FSCK	KY	08590	x	BS	FSNH	HT
08500	x	0	FSCD	DR	08593	x		MSSS	SF
08506	a		FSNY	TE	08594	x		MSSC	CA
08507	a		MSSR	RG	08595	x		FSCD	DR
08509	a	F	FSNT	TI	08597	x		FSCN	TO
08510	a		FSNT	TI	08599	x		MSNC	CD
08511	a		FSCN	TO	08600	a	D	NKJD	EH
08512	a	F	FSCD	DR	08601	x	0	MSNB	BS
08514	a		FSCD	DR	08603	x		MSCH	BS
08516	a	D	FSCK	KY	08604	x	G	MSNE	DY
08517	a		MSCH	MR	08605	x		FSCK	KY
08519	a	BS	MSSB	BY	08607	x		FSCN	TO

08609	x		MSSW	WN	08695	x		MSNC	CD
08610	x		MSNB	BS	08696	a	**D**	MSSW	WN
08611	x		MSNL	LO	08697	x		MSNE	DY
08613	x		MSNA	AN	08698	a		MSSS	SF
08615	x		MSNA	AN	08699	x		MSNC	CD
08616	x		MSNB	BS	08700	a		MSCH	BS
08617	x		MSSW	WN	08701	x	**RX**	FSNH	HT
08619	x		MSNL	LO	08702	x		MSNC	CD
08622	x		FSSM	ML	08703	x		MSNA	AN
08623	x		FSCN	TO	08705	a		MSCH	MR
08624	x		MSNL	LO	08706	x		FSCK	KY
08625	x		MSSB	BY	08707	a		FSCK	KY
08627	a		MSSS	SF	08709	x		MSSS	SF
08628	x		MSSB	BY	08711	x		MSSC	CA
08629	x		MSSB	BY	08713	a		MSCH	MR
08630	x		FSSM	ML	08714	x		MSSC	CA
08632	x		FSNI	IM	08715	v		MSSS	SF
08633	x	**RX**	MSNC	CD	08718	x		FSSM	ML
08635	x		MSNC	CD	08720	a	**D**	FSSM	ML
08641	xz	**D**	MSSL	LA	08721	x	**0**	MSNL	LO
08642	x*	**0**	NKJH	EH	08723	x		FSCN	TO
08643	xz	**D**	MSSA	BR	08724	x		MSSS	SF
08644	xz	**M**	MSSL	LA	08730	x	**0**	FSSM	ML
08645	xz	**D**	MSSL	LA	08731	x		FSSM	ML
08646	x	**F**	FSWL	LE	08733	x		FSSM	ML
08648	x*	**D**	MSSW	WN	08734	x		MSNB	BS
08649	x	**D**	NKJH	SU	08735	x		FSSM	ML
08651	xz	**D**	MSSO	OC	08737	x	**F**	MSNC	CD
08653	x*		MSSO	OC	08738	x	**D**	FSSM	ML
08655	x*	**F**	MSSS	SF	08739	x		MSNC	CD
08661	a		FSNL	NL	08740	x	**F**	MSSS	SF
08662	x		FSCK	KY	08742	x		MSNC	CD
08663	a	**D**	MSSL	LA	08745	xz	**BS**	FSNL	NL
08664	x		FSWK	CF	08746	x	**D**	MSNB	BS
08665	x		FSNI	IM	08748	x§		MSSS	SF
08666	x		MSNL	LO	08750	x		MSSS	SF
08668	x		MSSA	BR	08751	x		MSNB	BS
08670	a		MSCH	SF	08752	x	**C**	MSSS	SF
08673	x	**10**	MSNL	LO	08754	x		FSSI	IS
08675	x	**F**	FSSA	AY	08755	x		FSSM	ML
08676	x		MSNL	LO	08756	x	**D**	FSWL	LE
08677	x		MSSW	WN	08757	x	**D**	MSSC	CA
08682	x		FSCD	DR	08758	x		MSSS	SF
08683	x		MSSB	BY	08762	x		FSSI	IS
08685	x		MSSC	CA	08765	xn	**D**	MSNB	BS
08689	a		MSSS	SF	08767	x		MSSS	SF
08690	x		MSNU	CL	08768	x		MSNU	CL
08691	x	**G**	FSNT	TI	08770	a	**D**	FSWK	CF
08692	x		MSNC	CD	08772	x	**G**	MSSS	SF
08693	x		FSSM	ML	08773	x		FSCN	TO
08694	x		MSNA	AN	08775	x		MSSS	SF

08776	a	**D**	FSCK	KY	08877	x	**D**	FSCD	DR
08780	x		FSWL	LE	08878	x		MSCH	BS
08782	a		FSCK	KY	08879	x		FSNT	TI
08783	x		FSCK	KY	08880	x		FSNT	TI
08784	x		MSNC	CD	08881	x	**D**	FSSM	ML
08786	a		FSWK	CF	08882	x		FSSB	AB
08788	x		MSNE	DY	08883	x	**0**	FSSM	ML
08790	x		MSNL	LO	08884	x		MSNA	AN
08792	x		MSSL	LA	08886	x		FSNH	HT
08793	a	**0**	FSSB	AB	08887	x		MSSW	WN
08795	x	**D**	FSWK	CF	08888	xz	**R**	FSNH	HT
08798	x		FSWL	LE	08890	x	**D**	MSSW	WN
08799	x		MSNA	AN	08891	x		MSNL	LO
08801	x		MSSL	LA	08892	x*	**D**	NKJD	EH
08802	x		FSNH	HT	08893	x	**D**	MSNB	BS
08805	x	**FO**	MSNB	BS	08894	x		MSNA	AN
08806	a	**F**	FSCK	KY	08895	x		FSWK	CF
08807	x		MSSB	BY	08896	x		FSWL	LE
08809	x		MSNA	AN	08897	x	**D**	MSSA	BR
08810	a		MSSN	NC	08899	x		MSNE	DY
08811	a*		MSCH	SF	08900	x	**D**	MSNA	AN
08813	a	**D**	FSCD	DR	08901	xn		MSNB	BS
08815	x		MSNA	AN	08902	x		MSNA	AN
08817	x	**BS**	MSNA	AN	08903	x		FSCD	DR
08818	x		FSWK	CF	08904	x		MSSO	OC
08819	x	**D**	MSSL	LA	08905	x		MSSR	RG
08823	a		MSCH	CD	08906	x		FSNY	TE
08824	a	**F**	FSCD	DR	08907	x	**0**	MSNC	CD
08825	a		MSSO	OC	08908	xz		FSNL	NL
08826	a		MSNU	CL	08909	x		MSSS	SF
08827	a		MSNU	CL	08910	x		MSNU	CL
08828	a		MSSS	SF	08911	x	**D**	MSNU	CL
08829	a		FSCN	TO	08912	x		MSNU	CL
08830	x*		FSWK	CF	08913	x	**D**	MSNA	AN
08834	x	**F**	MSSS	SF	08914	x		MSSB	BY
08837	x*	**D**	MSSO	OC	08915	x	**F**	MSNL	LO
08842	x		MSNE	DY	08918	x	**D**	MSNA	AN
08844	x		MSNU	CL	08919	x		FSNT	TI
08845	x*	**D**	FSWK	CF	08920	x	**F**	MSNB	BS
08847	x*		NKJD	EH	08921	x		MSNC	CD
08849	x		MSSL	LA	08922	x	**D**	FSSM	ML
08853	xr		FSSM	ML	08923	x	**F**	MSSS	SF
08854	x*		NKJH	SU	08924	x	**D**	MSSR	RG
08855	x		FSSB	AB	08925	x		MSNA	AN
08856	x		MSNA	AN	08926	x		MSSW	WN
08865	x		MSSC	CA	08927	x		MSSB	BY
08866	x		MSCH	DR	08928	x	**FR**	MSSN	NC
08867	x	**0**	FSNY	TE	08931	x		FSNH	HT
08869	x	**G**	MSSN	NC	08932	x		FSWK	CF
08872	x	**D**	MSNA	AN	08933	x*	**0**	NKJD	EH
08873	x	**M**	MSSS	SF	08934	x		MSSW	WN

08937	x	D	MSSL	LA	08950	x	I	FSNL	NL
08938	xr	0	FSSM	ML	08951	x	D	MSNA	AN
08939	x		MSNA	AN	08952	x		FSSM	ML
08940	x		NKJD	EH	08953	x	D	MSSL	LA
08941	x		MSSL	LA	08954	x	F	MSSL	LA
08942	x		FSWK	CF	08955	x		MSSL	LA
08944	x	D	MSSO	OC	08956	x		MSSS	SF
08946	x	D	MSSR	RG	08957	x		MSSS	SF
08947	x		MSSO	OC	08958	x		MSSS	SF
08948	x		MSSO	OC					

Names:

08562	The Doncaster Postman	08772	CAMULODUNUM
08578	Libert Dickinson	08869	The Canary
08633	The Sorter	08888	Postman's Pride
08701	GATESHEAD TMD 1852 – 1991	08950	Neville Hill 1st

Class 08/9. Fitted with cut-down cab and headlight for Cwmmawr branch.

08993	(08592)	x		FSWL	LE	ASHBURNHAM
08994	(08462)	a	FR	FSWL	LE	GWENDRAETH
08995	(08687)	a	FC	FSWL	LE	KIDWELLY

CLASS 09   BR SHUNTER   0-6-0

Built: 1959 – 62 by BR at Darlington or Horwich Works.
Engine: English Electric 6KT of 298 kW (400 hp) at 680 rpm.
Main Generator: English Electric 801.
Traction Motors: English Electric 506.
Max. Tractive Effort: 111 kN (25000 lbf).
Cont. Tractive Effort: 39 kN (8800 lbf) at 11.6 mph.
Power At Rail: 201 kW (269 hp).
Brake Force: 19 t.   **Length over Buffers:** 8.92 m.
Weight: 50 t.   **Wheel Diameter:** 1372 mm.
Max. Speed: 27 mph.   **RA:** 5.

Formerly numbered 3665 – 71, 3719 – 21, 4099 – 4114.

CLASS 09/0. Built as Class 09.

09001		FSWK	CF		09014	D	FSCK	KY
09003		NKJH	SU		09015	D	FSWK	CF
09004		NKJH	SU		09016	D	NKJH	SU
09005	D	FSCK	KY		09018		NKJH	SU
09006		NKJH	SU		09019	D	NKJH	SU
09007		NKJH	SU		09020		NKJH	SU
09008	D	FSNT	TI		09021		NKJH	SU
09009	D	NKJH	SU		09022		NKJH	SU
09010	D	NKJH	SU		09023		NKJH	SU
09011	D	NKJH	SU		09024	D	NKJH	SU
09012	D	NKJH	SU		09025		NKJH	SU
09013	D	FSNT	TI		09026	D	NKJH	SU

Names:

09008	Sheffield Childrens Hospital	09012	Dick Hardy
09009	Three Bridges C.E.D.	09026	William Pearson

CLASS 09/1. Converted from Class 08. 90 V electrical equipment.

09101	(08833)	D	MSSR	RG
09102	(08832)	D	MSNC	CD
09103	(08766)	D	FSNY	TE
09104	(08749)	D	FSCN	TO
09105	(08835)	D	FSWK	CF
09106	(08759)	D	FSNT	TE

CLASS 09/2. Converted from Class 08. 100 V electrical equipment.

09201	(08421)	D	FSCN	TO
09202	(08732)	D	FSSM	ML
09203	(08781)	D	FSWK	CF
09204	(08717)	D	FSNY	TE

CLASS 20   ENGLISH ELECTRIC TYPE 1   Bo – Bo

Built: 1957 – 68 by English Electric Company at Vulcan Foundry, Newton le Willows or Robert Stephenson & Hawthorn, Darlington. 20001 – 128 were originally built with disc indicators whilst 20129 – 228 were built with four character headcode panels.
Engine: English Electric 8SVT Mk. II of 746 kW (1000 hp) at 850 rpm.
Main Generator: English Electric 819/3C.
Traction Motors: English Electric 526/5D (20001 – 48) or 526/8D (others).
Max. Tractive Effort: 187 kN (42000 lbf).
Cont. Tractive Effort: 111 kN (25000 lbf) at 11 mph.

Power At Rail: 574 kW (770 hp).	**Length over Buffers:** 14.25 m.
Brake Force: 35 t.	**Wheel Diameter:** 1092 mm.
Design Speed: 75 mph.	**Weight:** 73.5 t.
Max. Speed: 60 mph.	**RA:** 5.

Train Brakes: Air & vacuum.
Multiple Working: Blue Star Coupling Code.

Formerly numbered in series 8007 – 8195, 8314 – 8315.

CLASS 20/0. BR-owned Locomotives.

20007	st		TAKB	BS	20075	st	TAKB	BS (S)
20016	st		FCXX	TO (S)	20081	st	FCXX	TO (S)
20032	s		TAKB	BS	20082	st	FCXX	TO (U)
20046			FMXX	TE (U)	20087	st	CDJB	BS
20055	st		FCXX	TO (U)	20090	st **FR**	CDJX	TO (U)
20057	st		FCXX	TO (S)	20092	**CS**	CDJB	BS
20059	st **FR**		FCXX	TO (S)	20094	st	FMXX	TE (U)
20066			CDJB	BS	20096		FMXX	TE (U)
20071	st		FCXX	TO (U)	20104	st **FR**	TAKB	BS (S)
20072	st		TAKX	KN (U)	20106	st	TAKX	BS
20073	st		FCXX	SP (U)	20117	st	TAKX	KN (U)

20118	**FR**	CDJB	BS	20165	**FR**	CDJB	BS
20121	st	TAKX	KN (U)	20168	st	FCXX	TO (S)
20128	st	TAKB	BS	20169	st **CS**	CDJB	BS
20131	st	TAKB	BS (S)	20177	st	FCXX	TO (U)
20132	st **FR**	CDJB	BS	20186	st	FCXX	TO (U)
20135	st	FCXX	TO (U)	20187	st	TAKB	BS
20137	**FR**	CDJB	BS	20190	st	TAKX	KN (U)
20138	**FR**	CDJB	BS	20195	s	FCXX	TO (U)
20142	st	FCXX	TO (U)	20214	st	FMXX	TE (U)
20151	st	FCXX	TO (U)	20215	st **FR**	TAKX	KN (U)
20154	st	FCXX	TO (U)				

CLASS 20/9. Privately-owned by Hunslet – Barclay Ltd.

Used on summer weedkilling trains. Stored at Kilmarnock during the winter.
Non-standard Liveries: 20901 – 6 are in Hunslet – Barclay two-tone grey livery with red lettering.

20901	(20041)	t	**0**	XYPD	HB	NANCY
20902	(20060)		**0**	XYPD	HB	LORNA
20903	(20083)		**0**	XYPD	HB	ALISON
20904	(20101)		**0**	XYPD	HB	JANIS
20905	(20225)	t	**0**	XYPD	HB	IONA
20906	(20219)		**0**	XYPD	HB	Kilmarnock 400

CLASS 26   BRCW TYPE 2   Bo – Bo

Built: 1958 – 59 by the Birmingham Rly Carriage & Wagon Co., Smethwick.
Engine: Sulzer 6LDA28 of 870 kW (1160 hp) at 750rpm.
Main Generator: Crompton Parkinson CG391A1.
Traction Motors: Crompton Parkinson C171A1 (26/0), C171D3 (26/1).
Max. Tractive Effort: 187 kN (42000 lbf).
Cont. Tractive Effort: 133 kN (30000 lbf) at 11.25 mph.
Power At Rail: 671 kW (900 hp).   **Length over Buffers:** 15.47 m.
Brake Force: 35 t.   **Wheel Diameter:** 1092 mm.
Design Speed: 80 mph.   **Weight:** 75 t (26/0), 74.5 t (26/1).
Max. Speed: 60 mph.   **RA:** 5 or 6.
Train Brakes: Air & vacuum.
Multiple Working: Blue Star Coupling Code.
Communication Equipment: Fitted with cab to shore radio-telephone.

Formerly numbered 5301 – 43 (except 26007 (5300) & 26028 (5320)).

CLASS 26/0. RA6.

26001	s	**G**	RAJE	IS	Eastfield		
26003	s	**C**	RAJE	IS	26006	s **FC**	RFJX	IS (S)
26005	s	**C**	RAJE	IS	26007	s **G**	RAJE	IS

CLASS 26/1. RA5.

26025		**C**	RFJX	IS (S)	26036	**C**	RFJX	IS (S)
26032		**FR**	RFJX	IS (S)	26037	**FR**	RFJX	IS (S)

CLASS 31   BRUSH TYPE 2   A1A – A1A

Built: 1957 – 62 by Brush Traction at Loughborough. 31102/5 – 7/10/25/34/44/418/50/61/544 retain two headcode lights. Others have roof-mounted headcode boxes. 31215 has headcode box one end only.
Engine: English Electric 12SVT of 1100 kW (1470 hp) at 850 rpm.
Main Generator: Brush TG160-48.
Traction Motors: Brush TM73-68.
Max. Tractive Effort: 160 kN (35900 lbf) (190 kN (42800 lbf)*).
Cont. Tractive Effort: 83 kN (18700 lbf) at 23.5 mph. (99 kN (22250 lbf) at 19.7 mph *.)

Power At Rail: 872 kW (1170 hp).	**Length over Buffers:** 17.30 m.
Brake Force: 49 t.	**Driving Wheel Diameter:** 1092 mm.
Design Speed: 90 (80*) mph.	**Centre Wheel Diameter:** 1003 mm.
Max. Speed: 60 mph (90 mph 31/4)	**Weight:** 107 – 111 t.
RA: 5 or 6.	**ETH Index (Class 31/4):** 66.

Train Brakes: Air & vacuum.
Multiple Working: Blue Star Coupling Code.
Communication Equipment: This class is in the process of being fitted with cab to shore radio-telephone.

Non standard liveries:

31413 is BR blue with yellow cabsides, a light blue stripe along the bottom of the body and a red band around the bottom of the cabs.

Formerly numbered 5518/20 – 5862 (not in order).

CLASS 31/1. Standard Design. RA5.

31102		C	CEJB	BS	31154	C	IWJC	CD
31105	*	C	CEJB	BS	31155	C	RDJB	BS
31106	*	C	CEJB	BS	31158	C	RDDJ	BS
31107		C	CEJB	BS	31159	C	IWJC	CD
31110		C	CEJB	BS	31160	F	RCWC	CD
31112	*	C	CEJB	BS	31163	C	IWJC	CD
31113		C	CEJB	BS	31164	FO	RDJW	BS
31116		C	IMJB	BS	31165	G	NKJW	SF
31119		C	IMJB	BS	31166	C	RDDJ	BS
31125		C	CEJB	BS	31171	FO	IMJW	BS
31126		C	IMJB	BS	31174	C	RDJB	BS
31128		FO	RDJW	BS	31178	C	RDJB	BS
31130		FC	FCFN	TO	31180	FR	NKJW	SF
31132		FO	RDJW	BS	31181	C	NKJW	SF
31134		C	IMJW	BS	31184	FO	IEJW	IM
31135		C	NKJS	SF	31185	C	RDJB	BS
31142		C	IWJC	CD	31186	C	RDJM	SF
31144		C	IWJC	CD	31187	C	RDJS	SF
31145		C	IMJW	BS	31188	C	RCJC	CD
31146	r	C	RDDJ	BS	31190	C	RCWC	CD
31147	r	C	RDDJ	BS	31191	C	NKJW	SF
31149		FR	IEJW	IM	31199	FC	FCFN	TO

31200	FC	FCFN	TO		31255	C	RCJC	CD
31201	FC	FCFN	TO		31263	C	RCWC	CD
31203	C	IWJC	CD		31268	C	NKJW	SF
31205	FR	IEJW	IM		31270	FC	RCWC	CD
31206	C	IWJC	CD		31271	FA	IHFB	BS
31207	C	RCJC	CD		31272	C	RCJC	CD
31209	FA	IMJW	BS		31273	C	RDJB	BS
31217	FC	RCWC	CD		31275	FC	FCFN	TO
31219	C	RDJM	SF		31276	FC	IEJW	IM
31224	C	NKJS	SF		31282	FR	RCWC	CD
31229	C	RCJC	CD		31285	C	RCJC	CD
31230 *	FO	RBJW	IM		31290	C	NKJS	SF
31232	C	IWJC	CD		31294	FA	IEJW	IM
31233	C	RCJC	CD		31296	FA	RCWC	CD
31234	FO	IMJW	BS		31301	FR	RCWC	CD
31235	C	IWJC	CD		31302	FP	FCFN	TO
31237	C	RDJB	BS		31304	FC	FCFN	TO
31238	C	RCJC	CD		31306	C	RCJC	CD
31242	C	RCJC	CD		31308	C	RDJB	BS
31247	FR	RBJW	IM		31312	FC	FCFN	TO
31248	FO	IMJW	BS		31317	FO	RDJW	BS
31250	C	NKJS	SF		31319	FC	FCFN	TO
31252	FO	IMJW	BS		31327	FR	RCWC	CD

Names:

31102	Cricklewood	31130	Calder Hall Power Station
31105	Bescot TMD	31146	Brush Veteran
31106	The Blackcountryman	31165	Stratford Major Depot
31107	John H Carless VC	31233	Severn Valley Railway
31116	RAIL 1981 – 1991		

CLASS 31/4. Equipped with Train Heating. RA6.
CLASS 31/5. Dedicated for Civil Engineer's Department Use. Train Heating Equipment isolated. RA6.

31403		IHFB	BS	
31405	M	CEJB	BS	Mappa Mundi
31407 (31507)	M	IHFB	BS	
31408		RCKC	CD	
31410	RR	RCKC	CD	Granada Telethon
31411 (31511)	D	IMJW	BS	
31512 (31412)	C	IWJB	BS	
31413	O	IMJW	BS	
31514 (31414)	C	IWJB	BS	
31415		CEJB	BS	
31516 (31416)	C	IWJB	BS	
31417	D	IHRB	BS	
31418		IMJW	BS	
31519 (31419)	C	IWJB	BS	
31420 (31172)	M	IHRB	BS	
31421 (31140)	RR	RCKC	CD	Wigan Pier
31422 (31522)	M	IHRB	BS	

31423 (31197)	**M** IHRB	BS	Jerome K. Jerome
31524 (31424)	**C** IWJB	BS	
31526 (31426)	**C** IWJB	BS	
31427 (31194)	IMJW	BS	
31530 (31430)	**C** IWJB	BS	Sister Dora
31531 (31431)	**C** IEJI	IM	
31432 (31153)	RCKC	CD	
31533 (31433)	**C** IWJB	BS	
31434 (31258)	IHRB	BS	
31435 (31179)	**C** IHFB	BS	
31537 (31437)	**C** IWJB	BS	
31438 (31139)	RCKC	CD	
31439 (31239)	**RR** RCKC	CD	North Yorkshire Moors Railway Railway
31541 (31441)	**C** IEJI	IM	
31442 (31251)	RCKC	CD	
31544 (31444)	**C** IEJI	IM	Keighley and Worth Valley
31545 (31445)	**C** IWJB	BS	
31546 (31446)	**C** IWJB	BS	
31547 (31447)	**C** IEJW	IM	
31548 (31448)	**C** IWJB	BS	
31549 (31449)	**C** IEJI	IM	
31450 (31133)	IXXS	BS (U)	
31551 (31451)	**C** IWJB	BS	
31552 (31452)	**C** IEJI	IM	
31553 (31453)	**C** IEJI	IM	
31554 (31454)	**C** IWJB	BS	
31455 (31555)	**RR** RCKC	CD	Our Eli
31556 (31456)	**C** IEJI	IM	
31457 (31169)	**D** IHRB	BS	
31558 (31458)	**C** IEJI	IM	
31459 (31256)	IHFB	BS	
31460 (31266)	CEJB	BS	
31461 (31129)	**D** IHFB	BS	
31462 (31315)	**D** CEJB	BS	
31563 (31463)	**C** RBJW	IM	
31465 (31565)	**RR** RCKC	CD	
31466 (31115)	**C** IHFB	BS	
31467 (31216)	CEJB	BS	
31468 (31568)	**C** RDJB	BS	
31569 (31469)	**C** RDJW	BS	

CLASS 33   BRCW TYPE 3   Bo–Bo

Built: 1960 – 62 by the Birmingham Railway Carriage & Wagon Company, Smethwick.
Engine: Sulzer 8LDA28 of 1160 kW (1550 hp) at 750 rpm.

Trainload Construction

Trainload Coal

Trainload Metals

Trainload Petroleum

Railfreight Distribution

▲Trainload Freight and Railfreight Distribution sub-sector markings as used on locomotives.

▼The last remaining Class 03 in service, No. 03079 at Sandown on 31st July 1992. *John Augustson*

▲ Class 08 No. 08856 acting as station pilot at Liverpool Lime Street on 16th July 1992. *Doug Birmingham*

▼ Class 20 No. 20169 on display at Worcester open day in the new Central Services livery on 2nd March 1993. *Hugh Ballantyne*

Civil-Link Class 26s Nos. 26003 & 26005 double-head the 'Cumbrian Tynesider' railtour over the Calder Valley line near Smithy Bridge on 13th March 1993.

Vincent Eastwood

Old Railfreight liveried Class 31s Nos. 31327 with red stripe and 31299 are pictured leaving Hull on 9th May 1992 with 6M30 the 17.35 Hull – Ryistone.

Ian A Lyall

▲ Class 31 No. 31407 in Mainline livery at Norton Bridge with a Doncaster – Wembley e.c.s. on 11th June 1992.   *Hugh Ballantyne*

▼ Class 37 No. 37414 'Cathays C&W Works 1846-1993' in its new Regional Railways guise at Ipswich on 17th April 1993.   *Iain C Scotchman*

Class 33 No. 33051 'Shakespeare Cliff' at Redhill with the 09.37 Woking – Godstone tip engineers train on 6th May 1993.

Chris Wilson

Trainload Metals liveried Class 37 No. 37883 passing through Cowran cutting on 20th June 1992 with a Hardendale – Lackenby lime train.

Kevin Conkey

The 15.23 Sheffield – St. Pancras is pictured passing beneath the cooling towers of Ratcliffe-on-Soar power station with power cars 43047 'Rotherham Enterprise' & 43072 in charge on 21st May 1992.   *Ian A Lyall*

Main Generator: Crompton Parkinson CG391B1.
Traction Motors: Crompton Parkinson C171C2.
Max. Tractive Effort: 200 kN (45000 lbf).
Cont. Tractive Effort: 116 kN (26000 lbf) at 17.5 mph.
Power At Rail: 906 kW (1215 hp).   **Length over Buffers:** 15.47 m.
Brake Force: 35 t.   **Wheel Diameter:** 1092 mm.
Design Speed: 85 mph.   **Weight:** 77.5 t (78.5 t Class 33/1).
Max. Speed: 60 mph.   **RA:** 6.
Train Heating: Electric (y isolated).   **ETH Index:** 48.
Train Brakes: Air & vacuum.
Multiple Working: Blue Star Coupling Code.
Communication Equipment: This class is in the process of being fitted with cab to shore radio-telephone.

Formerly numbered in series 6500 – 97 but not in order.

Class 33/0. Standard Design.

33002	y	**C**	NKJR	SL	Sea King
33008	y	**G**	NKJE	EH	Eastleigh
33012			NKJE	SL	
33019	e	**C**	NKJE	EH	Griffon
33021	e	**FA**	NKJR	SL	
33025	e	**C**	NKJE	EH	Sultan
33026	e	**C**	NKJR	SL	Seafire
33030	e	**C**	NKJE	EH	
33035	y	**N**	NKJE	EH	
33042	ys	**FA**	NKJR	SL	
33046	y	**C**	NKJE	EH	Merlin
33048	es		NKJR	SL	
33051	e	**C**	NKJE	EH	Shakespeare Cliff
33052	e		NKJR	SL	Ashford
33053	e	**FA**	NKJR	SL	
33057	ys	**C**	NKJM	SL	Seagull
33063	ys	**FA**	NKJR	SL	
33064	e	**FA**	NKJM	SL	
33065	e	**C**	NKJR	SL	Sealion

Class 33/1. Fitted with Buckeye Couplings & SR Multiple Working Equipment for use with SR EMUs, TC stock & class 73.

Also fitted with flashing light adaptor for use on Weymouth Quay line.

33109	e	**D**	NKJM	SL
33116	e	**D**	NKJE	EH

Class 33/2. Built to Former Loading Gauge of Hastings Line.

33201	es	**C**	NKJM	SL	
33202	ys	**C**	NKJM	SL	The Burma Star
33204	es	**FD**	MDIB	SL	
33206	es	**FD**	MDIB	SL	
33207	ys	**FA**	MDIB	SL	Earl Mountbatten of Burma
33208	es	**C**	NKJM	SL	
33211	es	**FD**	MDIB	SL	

CLASS 37   ENGLISH ELECTRIC TYPE 3   Co–Co

Built: 1960 – 5 by English Electric Company at Vulcan Foundry, Newton le Willows or Robert Stephenson & Hawthorn, Darlington. 37003 – 116/350/1/9 with the exception of 37019*/031/047/053/065*/072*/073/074/075*/100* (* one end only) retain box-type route indicators, the remainder having central headcode panels/marker lamps.
Engine: English Electric 12CSVT of 1300 kW (1750 hp) at 850 rpm.
Main Generator: English Electric 822/10G.
Traction Motors: English Electric 538/A.
Max. Tractive Effort: 245 kN (55500 lbf).
Cont. Tractive Effort: 156 kN (35000 lbf) at 13.6 mph.
Power At Rail: 932 kW (1250 hp).   **Length over Buffers:** 18.75 m.
Brake Force: 50 t.   **Wheel Diameter:** 1092 mm.
Design Speed: 90 mph.   **Weight:** 103 – 108 t.
Max. Speed: 80 mph.   **RA:** 5 or 7.
Train Heating: Electric (Class 37/4 only). **ETH Index:** 38
Train Brakes: Air & vacuum.
Multiple Working: Blue Star Coupling Code.
Communication Equipment: This class is in the process of being fitted with cab to shore radio-telephone.

a Vacuum brake isolated.

Formerly numbered 6600 – 8, 6700 – 6999 (not in order). 37271 – 4 are the second locos to carry these numbers. They were renumbered to avoid confusion with Class 37/3 locos.

Class 37/0. Unrefurbished Locos. Technical details as above. RA5.

37003	+	**C** IEJI	IM	
37004		**FM** RAJV	IS	
37009	+	**FD** MDSR	TI (U)	
37010		**C** IGJK	CF	
37012		**C** IGJK	CF	
37013	+	**F** MDSR	TI (U)	
37015	+	**FD** MDTT	TI	
37019	+	**FD** MDTT	TI	
37023		**C** NKJS	SF	Stratford
37025		**C** RAJV	IS	
37026 (37320)	+	**FD** MDTT	TI	Shapfell
37029	+	**FD** MDYX	CE (U)	
37031	+	**FD** IGJA	BR	
37032 (37353)	+	**FR** MDYX	TI (U)	
37035		**C** IGJK	CF	
37037 (37321)		**FM** IGJA	BR	
37038		**C** IGJK	CF	
37040		**FM** IGJA	BR	
37042	+	**FM** IGJA	BR	
37043 (37354)		**C** RAJV	IS	
37045 (37355)	+	**F** MDSR	TI (S)	
37046		**C** IGJK	CF	

37047	+	FD	NKJS	SF	
37048		FM	IGJA	BR	
37049		C	RBJI	IM	Imperial
37051		FM	RAJV	IS	
37053	+	FD	MDTT	TI	
37054		C	IGJK	CF	
37055	+	FD	NKJS	SF	
37057	+	BR	MDYX	TI (U)	
37058	+	C	IEJI	IM	
37059	+	FD	RBJW	IM	Port of Tilbury
37063	+	FD	RBJW	IM	
37065	+	FD	IGJA	BR	
37066	+	C	IISW	IS	
37068 (37356)	+	FD	MDTT	TI	Grainflow
37069	+	C	RAJV	IS	
37070		FD	MDYX	TI (U)	
37071	+	C	IISW	IS	
37072	+	D	IGJA	BR	
37073	+	FD	MDTT	TI	Fort William/An Gearasdan
37074	+	FD	IGJA	BR	
37075	+	F	MDTT	TI	
37077		FM	IGJA	BR	
37078	+	FM	IISA	IS	
37079 (37357)	+	FD	MDTT	TI	Medite
37080		FP	IISA	IS	
37083	+	C	RBJI	IM	
37087		C	RAJV	IS	
37088 (37323)		D	RAJV	IS	Clydesdale
37092		C	IGJK	CF	
37095	+	C	IEJI	IM	
37097		C	IGJK	CF	
37098	+	C	IGJK	CF	
37099 (37324)		FM	RAJV	IS	Clydebridge
37100	+	FM	IISW	IS	
37101	+	FD	IGJA	BR	
37104		C	IEJI	IM	
37106	+	C	RAJV	IS	
37107	+	FD	MDTT	TI	
37108 (37325)	+	F	MDTT	TI	
37109		FM	IGJA	BR	
37110	+	FD	MDTT	TI	
37111 (37326)		FM	RAJV	IS	Glengarnock
37113	+	FD	IISA	IS	Radio Highland
37114	+	C	RDKB	BS	City of Worcester
37116	+	BR	MDSR	TI (S)	
37128	+	BR	RBJW	IM	
37131	+	FD	MDTT	TI	
37133		C	IISA	IS	
37137 (37312)		FM	IGJA	BR	Clyde Iron
37138		FM	IGJA	BR	
37139	+	FC	RBJI	IM	

37140		C	NKJS	SF
37141		C	REJK	CF
37142		C	REJK	CF
37144	r	FA	RBJI	IM
37146		C	REJK	CF
37152 (37310)		I	IISA	IS
37153		C	RAJV	IS
37154	+	FD	MDTT	TI	Johnson Stevens Agencies
37156 (37311)	r	C	RAJV	IS	British Steel Hunterston
37158		C	REJK	CF
37162	+	D	RDKB	BS
37165 (37374)	+	C	RAJV	IS
37167	+	FC	RAJV	IS
37170	r	C	IISA	IS
37174		C	IGJK	CF
37175		C	IISA	IS
37178	+	FD	MDTT	TI
37184		C	RAJV	IS
37185	+	C	RDKB	BS	Lea & Perrins
37188		FP	RAJV	IS
37190 (37314)		FM	RFJX	GD (U)
37191		C	REJK	CF
37194	+	FD	NKFE	EH	British International Freight Association
37196		C	RAJV	IS
37197	+	C	REJK	CF
37198	+	C	NKJE	EH
37201		FM	RAJV	IS
37202		FM	RBJW	IM
37203		FM	IGJA	BR
37207		C	REJK	CF
37209		BR	MDYX	TI (U)
37211		FA	RAJV	IS
37212	+	FC	RAJV	IS
37213	+	FC	IGJA	BR
37214	+	FA	IISA	IS
37215		FP	RFJX	CF
37216	r +	G	RDJS	SF	Great Eastern
37217	+		RBJW	IM
37218	+	FD	MDTT	TI
37219	r		IGJA	BR
37220	+	FP	NKFE	EH
37221		I	IISA	IS
37222	+	FC	IGJA	BR
37223	+	FC	IGJA	BR
37225	+	FD	MDTT	TI
37227	+	FM	IGJA	BR
37229	+	FC	IGJA	BR
37230	+	C	REJK	CF
37232	r	C	RAJV	IS	The Institution of Railway Signal Engineers

37235		+	**F**	MDSR	TI (U)	
37238		+	**FD**	MDTT	TI	
37239		+	**FC**	IISW	IS	The Coal Merchants' Association of Scotland
37240		+	**C**	RAJV	IS	
37241			**FM**	FIJW	IM	
37242		+	**FD**	NKJS	SF	
37244		+	**FD**	NKJS	SF	
37245			**C**	NKFE	EH	
37248		+	**FM**	MDYX	TI (U)	
37250		+	**FM**	IISA	IS	
37251		+	**I**	IISA	IS	The Northern Lights
37252			**FD**	MDYX	TI (U)	
37254		+	**C**	REJK	CF	
37255		+	**FM**	RAJV	IS	
37258		+	**C**	REJK	CF	
37261		+	**FD**	MDTT	TI	Caithness
37262		+	**D**	IISA	IS	Dounreay
37263			**C**	REJK	CF	
37264			**C**	IGJK	CF	
37271	(37303)	+	**FD**	IEJW	IM	
37272	(37304)	+	**FD**	RBJW	IM	
37274	(37308)	+	**C**	NKJE	EH	
37275		+	**FM**	RAJV	IS	
37278		+	**FC**	MDSR	TI (U)	
37280		+	**FP**	MDSR	TI (U)	
37285		+	**F**	RBJW	IM	
37293		+	**FM**	NKFE	EH	
37294		+	**C**	RAJV	IS	
37298		+	**FD**	MDTT	TI	

Class 37/3. Unrefurbished locos fitted with regeared (CP7) bogies.
Details as Class 37/0 except:
Max. Tractive Effort: 250 kN (56180 lbf).
Cont. Tractive Effort: 184 kN (41250 lbf) at 11.4 mph.

37350	(37119)	+	**FP**	FPYI	IM	
37351	(37002)	+	**C**	RAJV	IS	
37358	(37091)		**F**	MDRT	TI	P & O Containers
37359	(37118)		**FP**	MDRT	TI	
37370	(37127)		**C**	NKJS	SF	
37371	(37147)	+	**C**	NKJS	SF	
37372	(37159)		**C**	IGJK	CF	
37373	(37160)		**FR**	MDSR	TI (U)	
37375	(37193)	+	**C**	NKJE	EH	
37376	(37199)	+	**FC**	NKJS	SF	
37377	(37200)	+	**C**	NKJE	EH	
37378	(37204)	+	**FD**	MDRT	TI	
37379	(37226)		**C**	NKJS	SF	
37380	(37259)		**FC**	NKFE	EH	
37381	(37284)	+	**FM**	MDRT	TI	
37382	(37145)		**FP**	FPYI	IM	

Class 37/4. Refurbished locos fitted with train heating. Main generator replaced by alternator. Regeared (CP7) bogies. Details as class 37/0 except:

Main Alternator: Brush BA1005A.
Max. Tractive Effort: 256 kN (57440 lbf).
Cont. Tractive Effort: 184 kN (41250 lbf) at 11.4 mph.
Power At Rail: 935 kW (1254 hp).
All have twin fuel tanks.

37401 (37268) r	**M**	MDRM	ML	Mary Queen of Scots
37402 (37274) r	**M**	RAJV	IS	Oor Wullie
37403 (37307) r	**FD**	MDRM	ML	Glendarroch
37404 (37286) r	**M**	RAJV	IS	Ben Cruachan
37405 (37282) r	**M**	MDRT	TI	Strathclyde Region
37406 (37295) r	**M**	MDRM	ML	The Saltire Society
37407 (37305) r	**M**	RCMC	CD	Loch Long
37408 (37289)	**BR**	RCMC	CD	Loch Rannoch
37409 (37270) r	**M**	MDRM	ML	Loch Awe
37410 (37273) r	**M**	MDRM	ML	Aluminium 100
37411 (37290)	**FD**	MDRL	LA	
37412 (37301)	**FD**	MDRL	LA	
37413 (37276) r	**FD**	MDRL	LA	Loch Eil Outward Bound
37414 (37287) r	**RR**	RCMC	CD	Cathays C&W Works
				1846 – 1993
37415 (37277) r	**M**	MDRT	TI	
37416 (37302) r	**M**	MDRL	LA	
37417 (37269) r	**M**	MDRT	TI	Highland Region
37418 (37271) r	**FP**	RCMC	CD	Pectinidae
37419 (37291) r	**M**	MDRT	TI	
37420 (37297) r	**M**	MDRT	TI	The Scottish Hosteller
37421 (37267) r	**FP**	RCMC	CD	
37422 (37266) r	**RR**	RCMC	CD	Robert F. Fairlie
	Locomotive Engineer 1831 – 1885			
37423 (37296) r	**M**	MDRM	ML	Sir Murray Morrison
	1873 – 1948 Pioneer of British Aluminium Industry			
37424 (37279) r	**M**	MDRM	ML	Isle of Mull
37425 (37292) r	**FA**	RCMC	CD	Sir Robert McAlpine/
				Concrete Bob (opp. sides)
37426 (37299) r	**M**	MDRT	TI	
37427 (37288) r	**FA**	RAJP	IS	Highland Enterprise
37428 (37281) r	**FP**	RAJP	IS	David Lloyd George
37429 (37300) r	**RR**	RCMC	CD	
37430 (37265) r	**M**	MDRM	ML	Cwmbrân
37431 (37272) r	**M**	FPCI	IM	

Class 37/5. Refurbished locos. Main generator replaced by alternator. Regeared (CP7) bogies. Details as class 37/4 except:

Max. Tractive Effort: 248 kN (55590 lbf).
All have twin fuel tanks.

37501 (37005)	**FM**	FIJI	IM
37502 (37082)	**FM**	FIJW	IM

37503 (37017)		**FM** RCLC	CD	British Steel Shelton
37504 (37039)		**FM** RCLC	CD	
37505 (37028)		**FP** IISA	IS	
37506 (37007)		**FM** FPTY	TE	British Steel Skinningrove
37507 (37036)		**FM** FPYX	IM	
37508 (37090)	s	**FM** FPCI	IM	
37509 (37093)		**FM** RCLC	CD	
37510 (37112)		**I** IISA	IS	
37511 (37103)		**FM** FPCI	IM	Stockton Haulage
37512 (37022)		**FM** FIJW	IM	Thornaby Demon
37513 (37056)		**FM** FIJI	IM	
37514 (37115)	s	**FM** FMPY	TE	
37515 (37064)	s	**FM** FIJI	IM	
37516 (37086)	s	**FM** FMPY	TE	
37517 (37018)	s	**FM** FIJI	IM	
37518 (37076)		**FM** FPCI	IM	
37519 (37027)		**FM** FIJI	IM	
37520 (37041)		**FM** FPYI	IM	
37521 (37117)		**FP** FPEK	CF	
37667 (37151)	as	**FP** FPFR	IM	
37668 (37257)	s	**FP** FPEK	CF	
37669 (37129)		**FD** MDRL	LA	
37670 (37182)		**FD** MDRL	LA	St. Blazey T&RS Depot
37671 (37247)		**FD** MDRL	LA	Tre Pol and Pen
37672 (37189)	s	**FD** MDRL	LA	Freight Transport Association
37673 (37132)		**FD** MDRL	LA	
37674 (37169)		**FD** MDRL	LA	
37675 (37164)	s	**FD** MDRL	LA	William Cookworthy
37676 (37126)		**FA** FPFR	IM	
37677 (37121)		**FA** FABI	IM	
37678 (37256)		**FA** FPFR	IM	
37679 (37123)		**FA** FPFR	IM	
37680 (37224)		**FA** FABI	IM	
37682 (37236)		**FA** FPYI	IM	
37683 (37187)		**F** IISA	IS	
37684 (37134)		**FA** FPYI	IM	Peak National Park
37685 (37234)		**FR** FPYX	IM (U)	
37686 (37172)		**FA** FPYI	IM	
37687 (37181)		**FA** FIJW	IM	
37688 (37205)		**FA** FPYI	IM	Great Rocks
37689 (37195)	s	**FC** FPYI	IM	
37690 (37171)		**FO** FCPA	IM	
37691 (37179)	s	**FO** FIJI	IM	
37692 (37122)	s	**FC** FCPA	IM	
37693 (37210)	s	**FC** FCPA	IM	Sir William Arrol
37694 (37192)	s	**FC** FPCI	IM	The Lass O' Ballochmyle
37695 (37157)	s	**FC** FCPA	IM	
37696 (37228)	s	**FC** FCPA	IM	
37697 (37243)	s	**FC** FPEK	CF	
37698 (37246)	s	**FC** FPYI	IM	
37699 (37253)		**FC** FPYI	IM	

Class 37/7. Refurbished locos. Main generator replaced by alternator. Regeared (CP7) bogies. Ballast weights added.

Details as class 37/4 except:
Main Alternator: GEC G564AZ (37796 – 803) Brush BA1005A (others).
Max. Tractive Effort: 276 kN (62000 lbf).
Weight: 120 t.   **RA:** 7.
All have twin fuel tanks.

37701	(37030)	s	**FC** FCKK	CF	
37702	(37020)	s	**FC** FCKK	CF	Taff Merthyr
37703	(37067)	s	**FC** FCKK	CF	
37704	(37034)	s	**FC** FCKK	CF	
37705	(37060)		**FP** FPFR	IM	
37706	(37016)		**FP** FPCI	IM	Conidae
37707	(37001)		**FP** FPCI	IM	
37708	(37089)		**FP** FPCI	IM	
37709	(37014)		**FP** FPFR	IM	
37710	(37044)		**FM** FPFR	IM	
37711	(37085)		**FM** FPCI	IM	
37712	(37102)		**F** FPCI	IM	Teesside Steelmaster
37713	(37052)		**FM** FPCI	IM	British Steel Workington
37714	(37024)		**FM** FPCI	IM	
37715	(37021)		**FM** FPCI	IM	
37716	(37094)		**FM** FPTY	TE	British Steel Corby
37717	(37050)		**FM** FPCI	IM	Stainless Pioneer
37718	(37084)		**FM** FPTY	TE	Hartlepool Pipe Mill
37719	(37033)		**FP** FPCI	IM	
37796	(37105)	s	**FC** FCKK	CF	
37797	(37081)	s	**FC** FCKK	CF	
37798	(37006)	s	**FC** FPCI	IM	
37799	(37061)	s	**FC** FCKK	CF	Sir Dyfed/County of Dyfed
37800	(37143)	s	**FC** FPCI	IM	Glo Cymru
37801	(37173)	s	**FC** FPCI	IM	
37802	(37163)	s	**FC** FCKK	CF	
37803	(37208)	s	**FC** FPCI	IM	
37883	(37176)		**FM** FPCI	IM	
37884	(37183)		**F** FPCI	IM	Gartcosh
37885	(37177)		**FM** FPCI	IM	
37886	(37180)		**FM** FPCI	IM	
37887	(37120)	s	**FC** FCKK	CF	Caerphilly Castle
					Castell Caerffili (opp. sides)
37888	(37135)		**FP** FPYX	IM	Petrolea
37889	(37233)		**FC** FCKK	CF	
37890	(37168)		**FP** FPFR	IM	
37891	(37166)		**FP** FPCI	IM	
37892	(37149)		**FP** FPFR	IM	Ripple Lane
37893	(37237)		**FP** FPCI	IM	
37894	(37124)	s	**FC** FCKK	CF	
37895	(37283)	s	**FC** FCKK	CF	
37896	(37231)	s	**FC** FCKK	CF	
37897	(37155)	s	**FC** FCKK	CF	

37898	(37186)	s	**FC** FCKK	CF	
37899	(37161)	s	**FC** FCKK	CF	County of West Glamorgan/ Sir Gorllewin Morgannwg

Class 37/9. Refurbished Locos. Fitted with manufacturers prototype power units and ballast weights. Main generator replaced by alternator. Details as class 37/0 except:
Engine: Mirrlees MB275T of 1340 kW (1800 hp) at 1000 rpm (37901 – 4), Ruston RK270T of 1340 kW (1800 hp) at 900 rpm (37905 – 6).
Main Alternator: Brush BA1005A (GEC G564, 37905/6).
Max. Tractive Effort: 279 kN (62680 lbf).
Cont. Tractive Effort: 184 kN (41250 lbf) at 11.4 mph.
Weight: 120 t.   **RA:** 7.
All have twin fuel tanks.

37901	(37150)		**FM** FMHK	CF	Mirrlees Pioneer
37902	(37148)		**FM** FMHK	CF	
37903	(37249)		**FM** FMMK	CF	
37904	(37125)		**FM** FMHK	CF	
37905	(37136)	s	**FM** FMMK	CF	Vulcan Enterprise
37906	(37206)	s	**FM** FMHK	CF	

CLASS 43   HST POWER CAR   Bo – Bo

Built: 1976 – 82 by BREL Crewe Works. Formerly numbered as coaching stock but now classified as locomotives. Include luggage compartment.
Engine: Paxman Valenta 12RP200L of 1680 kW (2250 hp) at 1500 rpm. (Mirrlees MB190 of 1680 kW (2250 hp)*.
Main Alternator: Brush BA1001B.
Traction Motors: Brush TMH68 – 46 or GEC G417AZ (43124 – 151/180). Frame mounted.
Max. Tractive Effort: 80 kN (17980 lbf).
Cont. Tractive Effort: 46 kN (10340 lbf) at 64.5 mph.
Power At Rail: 1320 kW (1770 hp).   **ETH:** Non standard 3-phase system.
Brake Force: **Length over Buffers:** 17.79 m.
Weight: 70 t.   **Wheel Diameter:** 1020 mm.
Max. Speed: 125 mph.   **RA:** 5.
Train Brakes: Air.
Multiple Working: With one other similar vehicle.
Communication Equipment: All equipped with driver – guard telephone and cab to shore radio-telephone.

§ Modified to be able to remotely control a class 91 locomotive and to be remotely controlled by a class 91 locomotive.

43002	**I** IWRP	PM	Top of the Pops
43003	**I** IWRP	PM	
43004	**I** IWRP	PM	Swan Hunter
43005	**I** IWRP	PM	
43006	**I** IWRP	LA	
43007	**I** IWRP	LA	
43008	**I** IWRP	LA	
43009	**I** IWRP	PM	

43010	I	IWRP	PM	
43011	I	IWRP	PM	Reader 125
43012	I	IWRP	PM	
43013 §	I	ICCS	EC	
43014 §	I	ICCS	EC	
43015	I	IWRP	PM	
43016	I	IWRP	PM	Gwyl Gerddi Cymru 1992
				Garden Festival Wales 1992
43017	I	IWRP	PM	
43018	I	IWRP	PM	
43019	I	IWRP	PM	Dinas Abertawe/City of Swansea
43020	I	IWRP	LA	
43021	I	IWRP	LA	
43022	I	IWRP	LA	
43023	I	IWRP	LA	County of Cornwall
43024	I	IWRP	LA	
43025	I	IWRP	LA	
43026	I	IWRP	LA	City of Westminster
43027	I	IWRP	LA	
43028	I	IWRP	LA	
43029	I	IWRP	LA	
43030	I	IWRP	PM	
43031	I	IWRP	PM	
43032	I	IWRP	PM	The Royal Regiment of Wales
43033	I	IWRP	PM	
43034	I	IWRP	PM	
43035	I	IWRP	PM	
43036	I	IWRP	PM	
43037	I	IWRP	PM	
43038	I	IECP	NL	National Railway Museum
				The First Ten Years 1975 – 1985
43039	I	IECP	NL	
43040	I	IWRP	PM	Granite City
43041	I	IWRP	PM	City of Discovery
43042	I	IWCP	LA	
43043	I	IMLP	NL	
43044	I	IMLP	NL	
43045	I	IMLP	NL	The Grammar School Doncaster AD 1350
43046	I	IMLP	NL	
43047	I	IMLP	NL	Rotherham Enterprise
43048	I	IMLP	NL	
43049	I	IMLP	NL	Neville Hill
43050	I	IMLP	NL	
43051	I	IMLP	NL	The Duke and Duchess of York
43052	I	IMLP	NL	City of Peterborough
43053	I	IMLP	NL	County of Humberside
43054	I	IMLP	NL	
43055	I	IMLP	NL	
43056	I	IMLP	NL	University of Bradford
43057	I	IMLP	NL	Bounds Green
43058	I	IMLP	NL	

43059	I	IMLP	NL	
43060	I	IMLP	NL	County of Leicestershire
43061	I	IMLP	NL	City of Lincoln
43062	I	ICCS	EC	
43063	I	ICCS	EC	
43064	I	IMLP	NL	City of York
43065 §	I	ICCS	EC	
43066	I	IMLP	NL	
43067 §	I	ICCS	EC	
43068 §	I	ICCS	EC	
43069	I	ICCS	EC	
43070	I	ICCS	EC	
43071	I	ICCS	EC	
43072	I	IMLP	NL	
43073	I	IMLP	NL	
43074	I	IMLP	NL	
43075	I	IMLP	NL	
43076	I	IMLP	NL	BBC East Midlands Today
43077	I	IMLP	NL	County of Nottingham
43078	I	ICCS	EC	Shildon County Durham
43079	I	ICCS	EC	
43080 §	I	ICCS	EC	
43081	I	IMLP	NL	
43082	I	IMLP	NL	
43083	I	IMLP	NL	
43084 §	I	ICCS	EC	County of Derbyshire
43085	I	IMLP	NL	City of Bradford
43086	I	ICCP	NL	
43087	I	ICCP	NL	
43088	I	ICCP	NL	
43089	I	ICCP	NL	
43090	I	ICCS	EC	
43091	I	ICCS	EC	Edinburgh Military Tattoo
43092	I	ICCS	EC	Highland Chieftan
43093	I	ICCS	EC	York Festival '88
43094	I	ICCS	EC	
43095	I	IECP	NL	
43096	I	IECP	NL	The Queens Own Hussars
43097	I	ICCS	EC	
43098	I	ICCS	EC	
43099	I	ICCS	EC	
43100	I	ICCS	EC	Craigentinny
43101	I	ICCP	NL	
43102	I	ICCP	NL	
43103	I	ICCP	NL	John Wesley
43104	I	IECP	NL	
43105	I	IECP	NL	Hartlepool
43106	I	IECP	NL	Songs of Praise
43107	I	IECP	NL	
43108	I	IECP	NL	
43109	I	IECP	NL	Yorkshire Evening Press

43110	I	IECP	NL	Darlington
43111	I	IECP	NL	
43112	I	IECP	NL	
43113	I	IECP	NL	City of Newcastle-upon-Tyne
43114	I	IECP	NL	National Garden Festival Gateshead 1990
43115	I	IECP	NL	Yorkshire Cricket Academy
43116	I	IECP	NL	City of Kingston Upon Hull
43117	I	IECP	NL	
43118	I	IECP	NL	Charles Wesley
43119	I	IECP	NL	
43120	I	IECP	NL	
43121	I	ICCP	NL	West Yorkshire Metropolitan County
43122	I	ICCP	NL	South Yorkshire Metropolitan County
43123 §	I	ICCS	EC	
43124	I	ICCP	PM	
43125	I	IWRP	PM	
43126	I	IWRP	PM	City of Bristol
43127	I	IWRP	PM	
43128	I	IWRP	PM	
43129	I	IWRP	PM	
43130	I	ICCP	PM	Sulis Minerva
43131	I	IWRP	PM	
43132	I	ICCP	PM	Worshipful Company of Carmen
43133	I	IWRP	PM	
43134	I	IWRP	PM	County of Somerset
43135	I	IWRP	PM	
43136	I	IWRP	PM	
43137	I	IWRP	PM	
43138	I	ICCP	PM	
43139	I	IWRP	PM	
43140	I	IWRP	OO	
43141	I	IWCP	OO	
43142	I	IWCP	OO	
43143	I	IWRP	LA	
43144	I	IWCP	OO	
43145	I	IWCP	OO	
43146	I	IWCP	OO	
43147	I	IWCP	OO	The Red Cross
43148	I	IWRP	OO	
43149	I	IWRP	PM	B.B.C. Wales Today
43150	I	IWRP	PM	Bristol Evening Post
43151	I	IWRP	PM	
43152	I	IWRP	LA	St. Peters School York AD 627
43153	I	ICCP	LA	University of Durham
43154	I	ICCP	LA	
43155	I	ICCP	LA	B.B.C. Look North
43156	I	ICCP	LA	
43157	I	ICCP	LA	Yorkshire Evening Post
43158	I	ICCP	LA	
43159	I	ICCP	LA	
43160	I	ICCP	LA	Storm Force

43161	I	ICCP	LA	Reading Evening Post
43162	I	ICCP	LA	Borough of Stevenage
43163	I	IWRP	LA	
43164	I	IWRP	LA	
43165	I	IWRP	LA	
43166	I	IWRP	LA	
43167 * I		IWRP	PM	
43168 * I		IWRP	PM	
43169 * I		IWRP	PM	The National Trust
43170 * I		ICCP	PM	
43171	I	IWRP	LA	
43172	I	IWRP	LA	
43173	I	IWRP	LA	
43174	I	IWRP	LA	
43175	I	IWRP	LA	
43176	I	IWRP	LA	
43177	I	IWRP	LA	
43178	I	IWRP	LA	
43179	I	IWRP	LA	Pride of Laira
43180	I	ICCP	NL	
43181	I	IWRP	LA	
43182	I	IWRP	LA	
43183	I	IWRP	LA	
43184	I	IWRP	LA	
43185	I	IWRP	LA	Great Western
43186	I	IWRP	LA	Sir Francis Drake
43187	I	IWRP	LA	
43188	I	IWRP	LA	City of Plymouth
43189	I	IWRP	LA	
43190	I	IWRP	LA	
43191	I	IWRP	LA	Seahawk
43192	I	IWRP	LA	City of Truro
43193	I	ICCP	LA	
43194	I	ICCP	LA	
43195	I	ICCP	LA	
43196	I	ICCP	LA	The Newspaper Society Founded 1836
43197	I	ICCP	LA	
43198	I	ICCP	NL	

CLASS 47   BRUSH TYPE 4   Co – Co

Built: 1963 – 67 by Brush Traction, Loughborough or BR Crewe Works.
Engine: Sulzer 12LDA28C of 1920 kW (2580 hp) at 750 rpm.
Main Generator: Brush TG160-60 Mk2, TG 160-60 Mk4 or TM172-50 Mk1.
Traction Motors: Brush TM64-68 Mk1 or Mk1A (axle hung).
Max. Tractive Effort: 267 kN (60000 lbf).(245 kN (55000 lbf) 47401 – 18)
Cont. Tractive Effort: 133 kN (30000 lbf) at 26 mph.
Power At Rail: 1550 kW (2080 hp).   **Length over Buffers:** 19.38 m.
Brake Force: 61 t.   **Wheel Diameter:** 1143 mm.
Design Speed: 95 mph.   **Weight:** 120.5 – 125 t.
Max. Speed: various.   **RA:** 6 or 7.

Train Brakes: Air & vacuum.
Multiple Working: Not equipped (Blue Star Coupling Code*).
ETH Index (47/4 & 47/7): 66 (75§).
Communication Equipment: Cab to shore radio-telephone.
Non standard livery: 47803 is grey, red and yellow.

a Vacuum brake isolated.

Formerly numbered 1100 – 11, 1500 – 1999 not in order. 47299 was also
previously 47216. 47300 was previously 47468.

Class 47/0. Built with train heating boiler. RA6. Max Speed 75 mph.

47004	**FA**	IGJW	OC	
47016	**FO**	IGJW	OC	
47019	**FO**	IGJW	OC	
47033 a + **FD**		MDCT	TI	
47049 + **FD**		MDDT	TI	
47050 a + **FD**		MDYX	TI (U)	
47051 a + **FD**		MDCT	TI	
47052	**FD**	MDAT	TI	
47053 a + **FD**		MDDT	TI	Cory Brothers 1842-1992
47060 a	**FD**	MDYX	TI (U)	Halewood Silver Jubilee 1988
47063	**FA**	MDYX	TI (U)	
47079	**FD**	MDWT	TI	
47085 +	**F**	MDDT	TI	
47095 +	**FD**	MDYX	TI (U)	
47105		IGJW	OC	
47108		IGJW	OC	
47114 a + **FA**		MDDT	TI	
47121		IGJW	OC	
47125 +	**FD**	MDDT	TI	
47142	**FR**	MDWT	TI	The Sapper
47144 a + **FD**		MDDT	TI	
47145		MDWT	TI	
47146 a		MDWT	TI	
47147	**FD**	MDAT	TI	
47150 +	**FD**	MDDT	TI	
47152 +	**FD**	MDDT	TI	
47156 a + **FD**		MDDT	TI	
47157	**F**	MDWT	TI	
47186 a + **FD**		MDDT	TI	Catcliffe Demon
47187	**FD**	MDAT	TI	
47188 a + **FD**		MDDT	TI	
47190	**FP**	MDYX	TI (U)	
47193	**FP**	MDWT	TI	Lucinidae
47194 +	**FD**	MDDT	TI	Carlisle Currock Quality Approved
47196	**FP**	MDWT	TI	
47197	**FP**	MDWT	TI	
47200 a + **FD**		MDDT	TI	
47201 +	**FD**	MDDT	TI	
47204 a + **FD**		MDDT	TI	
47205 +	**FD**	MDDT	TI	

47206	**FD**	MDWT	TI
47207	**FD**	MDAT	TI	Bulmers of Hereford
47209 +	**FD**	MDDT	TI	Herbert Austin
47210 +	**FD**	MDDT	TI
47211 +	**FD**	MDDT	TI
47212 +	**FP**	MDWT	TI
47213 +	**F**	MDDT	TI
47214	**FD**	MDYX	TI (U) Distillers MG
47217 a +	**FD**	MDDT	TI
47218 +	**FD**	MDDT	TI	United Transport Europe
47219 a +	**FD**	MDCT	TI	Arnold Kunzler
47220	**F0**	MDYX	TI (U)
47221 +	**FP**	MDWT	TI
47222 a +	**FD**	MDCT	TI
47223 +	**FP**	MDWT	TI
47224 +	**FP**	MDWT	TI
47225	**FD**	MDYX	TI (U)
47226 a +	**FD**	MDDT	TI
47228 +	**FD**	MDDT	TI
47229 a +	**FD**	MDDT	TI
47231	**FD**	MDWT	TI	The Silcock Express
47234 +	**FD**	MDDT	TI
47236 a +	**FD**	MDCT	TI
47237 a +	**FD**	MDCT	TI
47238	**FD**	MDAT	TI	Bescot Yard
47241 a +	**FD**	MDDT	TI
47245 +	**FD**	MDDT	TI
47249	**FR**	MDWT	TI
47256	**FD**	MDWT	TI
47258 +	**FD**	MDDT	TI
47270		MDWT	TI
47276 +	**FP**	MDWT	TI
47277	**FP**	MDWT	TI
47278	**FP**	MDWT	TI
47279	**FD**	MDAT	TI
47280 a +	**FD**	MDCT	TI	Pedigree
47281 +	**FD**	MDDT	TI
47283	**FD**	MDWT	TI	Johnnie Walker
47284 +	**FD**	MDDT	TI
47285 a +	**FD**	MDCT	TI
47286 a +	**F**	MDDT	TI
47287 +	**FD**	MDDT	TI
47288	**FD**	MDAT	TI
47289 a	**FD**	MDAT	TI
47290 a +	**FD**	MDDT	TI
47291 a +	**FD**	MDDT	TI	The Port of Felixstowe
47292 a +	**FD**	MDDT	TI
47293 a +	**FD**	MDDT	TI
47294 +	**FP**	MDWT	TI
47295 +	**FP**	MDYX	TI (S)
47296	**FD**	MDAT	TI

47297	a + **FD**	MDDT	TI	
47298	+ **FD**	MDDT	TI	Pegasus
47299	a + **FD**	MDDT	TI	

Class 47/3. Built without Train Heat. (except 47300). RA6. Max Speed 75 mph. All equipped with slow speed control.

47300	**C**	CEJB	BS	
47301	**FR**	MDAT	TI	
47302	a **FR**	MDAT	TI	
47303	a + **F**	MDDT	TI	
47304	a + **FD**	MDDT	TI	
47305	**FP**	MDAT	TI	
47306	a + **FD**	MDYX	TI (U)	
47307	+ **FD**	MDDT	TI	
47308	**F**	MDWT	TI	
47309	+ **FD**	MDDT	TI	The Halewood Transmission
47310	a + **FD**	MDCT	TI	Henry Ford
47312	a + **FD**	MDDT	TI	
47313	a + **FD**	MDCT	TI	
47314	a + **FD**	MDDT	TI	Transmark
47315	**C**	IGJO	OC	
47316	a + **FD**	MDCT	TI	
47317	**FD**	MDWT	TI	Willesden Yard
47318	**FD**	IWJD	CD	
47319	+ **FP**	FCCI	IM	Norşk Hydro
47320	**FO**	MDYX	ZC (U)	
47321	**F**	MDWT	TI	
47322	**FR**	MDWT	TI	
47323	a + **FD**	MDCT	TI	
47325	**FO**	MDYX	TI (U)	
47326	a + **FD**	MDCT	TI	
47328	+ **FD**	MDDT	TI	
47329	**C**	IWJD	CD	
47330	a + **FD**	MDDT	TI	Amlwch Freighter/ Trên Nwyddau Amlwch (Opp. Sides)
47331	**C**	IEJI	IM	
47332	**C**	CEJB	BS	
47333	**C**	CEJB	BS	Civil Link
47334	**C**	IWJD	CD	
47335	a + **FD**	MDDT	TI	
47336	+ **FP**	IEJW	IM	
47337	**FO**	MDWT	TI	
47338	a + **FD**	MDDT	TI	Warrington Yard
47339	**FD**	MDAT	TI	
47340	**C**	IWJD	CD	
47341	**C**	CEJB	BS	
47344	a + **F**	MDDT	TI	
47345	**FR**	MDWT	TI	
47346	**C**	RBJW	IM	
47347	a **FM**	MDAT	TI	
47348	**FO**	IMJC	BR	St. Christopher's Railway Home

47349	FD	MDYX	TI (U)	
47350	FO	MDWT	TI	
47351 a +	FD	MDDT	TI	
47352	C	MDWT	TI	
47353	C	CEJB	BS	
47354 a	FD	MDWT	TI	
47355 +	FD	MDDT	TI	
47356	FO	CEJB	BS	
47357	C	CEJB	BS	The Permanent Way Institution
47358	FO	IGJW	OC	
47359	FD	MDAT	TI	
47360 a +	FD	MDDT	TI	
47361 a +	FD	MDDT	TI	Wilton Endeavour
47362 a +	FD	MDCT	TI	
47363 +	F	MDDT	TI	
47364	C	NKJS	SF	
47365 +	FD	MDDT	TI	ICI Diamond Jubilee
47366	FO	IGJO	OC	
47367	FR	MDAT	TI	
47368	FP	IMJC	BR	Neritidae
47369	FP	MDWT	TI	
47370	FO	MDWT	TI	
47371	FO	MDWT	TI	
47372	C	CEJB	BS	
47375 a +	FD	MDDT	TI	Tinsley Traction Depot Quality Approved
47376		MDAT	TI	
47377 a	FD	MDAT	TI	
47378 a +	FD	MDDT	TI	
47379 +	FP	MDWT	TI	

Class 47/4. Equipped with train heating. RA7. Max Speed 95 (75§) mph.

47443	BR	PXLC	CD	North Eastern
47462	R	PXLC	CD	Cambridge Traction & Rolling Stock Depot
47463		PXLC	CD	
47467	BR	PXLC	CD	
47471	IO	PXLC	CD	Norman Tunna G.C.
47473	BR	IWJD	CD	
47474	R	PXLC	CD	Sir Rowland Hill
47475	RX	PXLC	CD	Restive
47476	R	PXLC	CD	Night Mail
47478		IWJD	CD	
47481	BR	PXLC	CD	
47482	BR	PXLC	CD	
47483	M	IMJC	BR	
47484	G	IGJW	OC	ISAMBARD KINGDOM BRUNEL
47485	BR	PXLC	CD	
47488	BR	PXLC	CD	
47489	R	PXLC	CD	Crewe Diesel Depot
47490 +	RX	PXLB	CD	Resonant

47491		+	RX	PXLB	CD	
47492			IO	PXLC	CD	
47500		+	RX	PXLB	CD	
47501			R	PXLC	CD	Craftsman
47503		+	RX	PXLB	CD	Heaton Traincare Depot
47513			BR	PXLC	CD	Severn
47517		+	RX	PXLB	CD	
47519			BR	PXLC	CD	
47520			M	IEJI	IM	
47521			N	PXLC	CD	
47522			R	PXLC	CD	Doncaster Enterprise
47523			M	PXLC	CD	
47524			M	PXLC	CD	
47525			IO	IWJD	CD	
47526			BR	NXXB	SF	
47528			M	PXLC	CD	The Queen's Own Mercian Yeomanry
47530			RX	PXLC	CD	
47531	(47974)	+	RX	PXLB	CD	
47532			RX	PXLC	CD	
47535			R	PXLC	CD	University of Leicester
47536			BR	PXLC	CD	
47537		+	RX	PXLB	CD	
47539			RX	PXLC	CD	
47541		+	RX	PXLB	CD	
47543			R	PXLC	CD	
47547			N	PXLC	CD	
47550			M	IEJW	IM	University of Dundee
47551	(47801)	+	RX	PXLB	CD	
47555	(47126)		IO	IMJC	BR	
47557	(47024)		M	PXLC	CD	
47558	(47027)		M	PXLC	CD	Mayflower
47559	(47028)	+	RX	PXLB	CD	
47562	(47672)	+	RX	PXLB	CD	
47564	(47038)		BR	PXLD	CD	
47565	(47039)		M	PXLC	CD	
47566	(47043)		M	PXLC	CD	
47567	(47044)		M	PXLC	CD	Red Star
47568	(47045)		RX	PXLC	CD	
47569	(47047)		R	PXLC	CD	The Gloucestershire Regiment
47572	(47168)		R	PXLC	CD	Ely Cathedral
47573	(47173)	+	RX	PXLB	CD	
47574	(47174)		R	PXLC	CD	Benjamin Gimbert G.C.
47575	(47175)		R	PXLC	CD	City of Hereford
47576	(47176)		RX	PXLC	CD	
47578	(47181)	+	RX	PXLB	CD	
47579	(47183)		N	NXXB	SF	James Nightall G.C.
47580	(47167)		BR	PXLC	CD	County of Essex
47581	(47169)	+	RX	PXLB	CD	
47582	(47170)		R	PXLC	CD	County of Norfolk

47583	(47172)		**N**	PXLC	CD	County of Hertfordshire
47584	(47180)		**M**	PXLC	CD	County of Suffolk
47587	(47263)		**N**	PXLC	CD	
47588	(47178)		**RX**	PXLC	CD	Resurgent
47592	(47171)		**BR**	PXLC	CD	County of Avon
47594	(47035)		**RX**	PXLC	CD	Resourceful
47596	(47255)		**N**	PXLC	CD	Aldeburgh Festival
47597	(47026)		**RX**	PXLC	CD	Resilient
47598	(47182)		**RX**	PXLC	CD	
47599	(47177)		**RX**	PXLC	CD	
47600	(47250)		**RX**	PXLC	CD	
47603	(47267)		**BR**	PXLC	CD	
47605	(47160)		**RX**	PXLC	CD	
47606	(47842)	+	**RX**	PXLB	CD	
47612	(47838)	+	**RX**	PXLB	CD	
47615	(47252)		**RX**	PXLC	CD	
47618	(47836)	+	**RX**	PXLB	CD	
47624	(47087)		**M**	PXLC	CD	
47625	(47076)		**RX**	PXLC	CD	Resplendent
47626	(47082)		**M**	PXLC	CD	ATLAS
47627	(47273)		**RX**	PXLC	CD	
47628	(47078)		**RX**	PXLC	CD	
47630	(47041)	+	**RX**	PXLB	CD	
47631	(47059)	+	**RX**	PXLB	CD	
47634	(47158)		**R**	PXLC	CD	Holbeck
47635	(47029)		**RX**	PXLC	CD	
47636	(47243)	+	**RX**	PXLB	CD	Restored
47640	(47244)		**R**	PXLC	CD	University of Strathclyde
47641	(47086)		**BR**	PXLD	CD	
47642	(47040)	+	**RX**	PXLB	CD	Resolute
47644	(47246)		**BR**	PXLD	CD	
47671	(47616)	§	**BR**	IEJI	IM	
47673	(47593)	§	**IO**	IEJI	IM	Galloway Princess
47674	(47604)	§	**BR**	IMJC	BR	Women's Royal Voluntary Service
47675	(47595)	§	**M**	IEJI	IM	Confederation of British Industry
47676	(47586)	§	**I**	IEJI	IM	Northamptonshire
47677	(47617)	§	**I**	IMJC	BR	University of Stirling

Class 47/7. TDM fitted. RA6. Max speed. 100 mph.

47701	(47493)	+	**N**	NTWH	EH	Old Oak Common Traction & Rolling Stock Depot
47702	(47504)	+	**N**	NTWH	EH	Saint Cuthbert
47703	(47514)	+	**R**	NTWH	EH	The Queen Mother
47704	(47495)	+	**RX**	PXLB	CD	
47705	(47554)	+	**N**	NTWH	EH	
47706	(47494)	+	**PS**	PXLB	CD	
47707	(47506)	+	**N**	PXLB	CD	Holyrood
47708	(47516)	+	**N**	PXLB	CD	Templecombe
47709	(47499)	+	**N**	PXLB	CD	

47710 (47496)	+ **N**	PXLB	CD	Capital Radio's Help a London Child
47711 (47498)	+ **N**	NXXB	SF	
47712 (47505)	+ **R**	PXLB	CD	Lady Diana Spencer
47714 (47511)	+ **N**	PXLB	CD	
47715 (47502)	+ **N**	NTWH	EH	Haymarket
47716 (47507)	+ **N**	NTWH	EH	Duke of Edinburgh's Award
47717 (47497)	+ **R**	NTWH	EH	

Class 47/4 continued.

47802 (47552)	+ **I**	IMJC	BR	
47803 (47553)	+ **O**	IMJC	BR	
47804 (47591)	+ **I**	IMJC	BR	Kettering
47805 (47650)	+ **I**	ILRA	BR	Bristol Bath Road
47806 (47651)	+ **I**	ILRA	BR	
47807 (47652)	+ **I**	ILRA	BR	
47808 (47653)	+ **I**	PXLB	BR	Samson
47809 (47654)	+ **I**	IBRA	BR	Finsbury Park
47810 (47655)	+ **I**	ILRA	BR	
47811 (47656)	+ **I**	ILRA	BR	
47812 (47657)	+ **I**	ILRA	BR	
47813 (47658)	+ **I**	ILRA	BR	
47814 (47659)	+ **I**	ILRA	BR	
47815 (47660)	+ **I**	ILRA	BR	
47816 (47661)	+ **I**	ILRA	BR	
47817 (47662)	+ **I**	ILRA	BR	
47818 (47663)	+ **M**	ILRA	BR	
47819 (47664)	+ **I**	IBRA	BR	
47820 (47665)	+ **I**	IBRA	BR	
47821 (47607)	+ **I**	IBRA	BR	Royal Worcester
47822 (47571)	+ **I**	ILRA	BR	
47823 (47610)	+ **I**	IBRA	BR	SS Great Britain
47824 (47602)	+ **M**	IMJC	BR	
47825 (47590)	+ **M**	ILRA	BR	Thomas Telford
47826 (47637)	+ **I**	ILRA	BR	
47827 (47589)	+ **I**	ILRA	BR	
47828 (47629)	+ **I**	ILRA	BR	
47829 (47619)	+ **M**	ILRA	BR	
47830 (47649)	+ **I**	ILRA	BR	
47831 (47563)	+ **M**	ILRA	BR	Bolton Wanderer
47832 (47560)	+ **M**	ILRA	BR	Tamar
47833 (47608)	+ **G**	IBRA	BR	Captain Peter Manisty RN
47834 (47609)	+ **I**	IBRA	BR	FIRE FLY
47835 (47620)	+ **I**	IBRA	BR	Windsor Castle
47839 (47621)	+ **I**	ILRA	BR	
47840 (47613)	+ **I**	IBRB	BR(S)	NORTH STAR
47841 (47622)	+ **I**	ILRA	BR	The Institution of Mechanical Engineers
47843 (47623)	+ **I**	IBRB	BR(S)	
47844 (47556)	+ **I**	ILRA	BR	Derby & Derbyshire Chamber of Commerce & Industry

47845	(47638)	+ I	ILRA	BR	County of Kent
47846	(47647)	+ I	ILRA	BR	THOR
47847	(47577)	+ I	ILRA	BR	
47848	(47632)	+ I	ILRA	BR	
47849	(47570)	+ M	ILRA	BR	
47850	(47648)	+ I	ILRA	BR	
47851	(47639)	+ I	IBRB(S)	BR	
47853	(47614)	+ M	ILRA	BR	
47971	(97480)	* BR	CDJB	BS	Robin Hood
47972	(97545)	CS	CDJB	BS	The Royal Army Ordnance Corps
47973	(97561)	M	CDJB	BS	Derby Evening Telegraph
47975	(47540)	* C	CDJB	BS	The Institution of Civil Engineers
47976	(47546)	* C	CDJB	BS	Aviemore Centre

CLASS 50   ENGLISH ELECTRIC TYPE 4   Co–Co

Built: 1967 – 68 by English Electric Co. at Vulcan Foundry, Newton le Willows.
Engine: English Electric 16CVST of 2010 kW (2700 hp) at 850 rpm.
Main Generator: English Electric 840/4B.
Traction Motors: English Electric 538/5A.
Max. Tractive Effort: 216 kN (48500 lbf).
Cont. Tractive Effort: 147 kN (33000 lbf) at 23.5 mph.
Power At Rail: 1540 kW (2070 hp).   **Length over Buffers:** 20.88 m.
Brake Force: 59 t.   **Wheel Diameter:** 1092 mm.
Design Speed: 105 mph.   **Weight:** 117 t.
Max. Speed: 100 mph.   **RA:** 6.
Train Heating: Electric. **ETH Index:** 61.
Train Brakes: Air & vacuum.
Multiple Working: Orange Square coupling code. (Within class only).
Communication Equipment: Cab to shore radio-telephone.
All equipped with slow speed control.

Formerly numbered 407, 433, 400.

50007	G	NWXA	LA	SIR EDWARD ELGAR
50033	N	NWXA	LA	Glorious
50050		NWXA	LA	

CLASS 56   BRUSH TYPE 5   Co–Co

Built: 1976 – 84 by Electroputere at Craiova, Romania (as sub contractors for Brush) or BREL at Doncaster or Crewe Works.
Engine: Ruston Paxman 16RK3CT of 2460 kW (3250 hp) at 900 rpm.
Main Alternator: Brush BA1101A.
Traction Motors: Brush TM73-62.
Max. Tractive Effort: 275 kN (61800 lbf).
Cont. Tractive Effort: 240 kN (53950 lbf) at 16.8 mph.
Power At Rail: 1790 kW (2400 hp).   **Length over Buffers:** 19.36 m.
Brake Force: 60 t.   **Wheel Diameter:** 1143 mm.
Design Speed: 80 mph.   **Weight:** 125 t.
Max. Speed: 80 mph.   **RA:** 7.

Train Brakes: Air.
Multiple Working: Red Diamond coupling code.
Communication Equipment: Cab to shore radio-telephone.
All equipped with slow speed control.

§ Derated to 1790 kW (2400 hp).
* Derated to 2060 kW (2800 hp).

56001	FA	FQXB	SL	Whatley
56003	F	FCXX	TO (S)	
56004		FCXX	TO (S)	
56005	FC	FCBN	TO	
56006	FC	FCBN	TO	
56007	FC	FCBN	TO	
56008		FCXX	TO (U)	
56009	FC	FCBN	TO	
56010		FCBN	TO	
56011	FR	FCBN	TO	
56012	FC	FCXX	TO (U)	
56013	FC	FCXX	TO (U)	
56014	FC	FCXX	TO	
56015	FC	FCXX	TO (U)	
56016	FC	FCXX	TO (U)	
56018	FC	FCBN	TO	
56019	FR	FCXX	TO (U)	
56020		FCXX	TO (U)	
56021	FC	FCBN	TO	
56022		FCXX	TO (U)	
56023	FC	FCDN	TO	
56024	FO	FCXX	TO (U)	
56025	FC	FCXX	TO (S)	
56026		FCXX	TO (U)	
56027	FC	FCDN	TO	
56028	FC	FCXX	TO (U)	West Burton Power Station
56029	FC	FCXX	TO (S)	
56030	FC	FCXX	TO (U)	
56031	C	NKJM	SL	Merehead
56032	FM	FMCK	CF	Sir De Morgannwg/ County of South Glamorgan
56033	FA	FASB	SL	
56034	FA	FMTY	TE	Castell Ogwr/Ogmore Castle
56035	FA	FASB	SL	
56036	C	NKJM	SL	
56037	FA	FASB	SL	Richard Trevithick
56038	FM	FMCK	CF	Western Mail
56039	FA	FQXB	SL	
56040	FM	FMCK	CF	Oystermouth
56041	FA	FASB	SL	
56043	FA	FMTY	TE	
56044	FM	FMCK	CF	Cardiff Canton Quality Assured
56045	FA	FMTY	TE	
56046	C	NKJM	SL	

THE PLATFORM 5
TRANSPORT BOOK CLUB

The Platform 5 Transport Book Club is a service for transport enthusiasts which enables members to order new Platform 5 titles before publication, at discounts of between 15% and 25% of the normal retail price. Unlike other book clubs, a small annual subscription fee of £1.50 is charged to cover the production and postage of a quarterly newsletter, but there is no obligation whatsoever to buy any books at any time. We like customers to buy our books because of their quality, not because of any obligation to a book club.

To illustrate the sort of discounts available, the following offer applied to German Railways Locomotives and Multiple Units 3rd edition before publication in June 1993:

Cover Price:.............................	£12.50
Less Book Club Member Discount:.............	£2.50
	£10.00
Plus 10% Contribution to Postage & Packing.....	£1.00
BOOK CLUB MEMBER PRICE................	**£11.00**

Even after our 10% postage and packing charge, this still represents a saving of £1.50 on the cover price.

Discounted prices will of course, only be available to Platform 5 Transport Book Club members, and will only be applicable if subscriptions are received by a certain date prior to publication, to be advised.

In addition, a discount on selected existing Platform 5 titles will occasionally be offered to Book Club members.

There is no limit to the number of copies of each book that may be ordered through the Platform 5 Transport Book Club.

Books ordered through the Platform 5 Transport Book Club will be despatched as soon as possible after publication.

Customers should be aware that although most new Platform 5 titles will be available via this service, some low-priced titles will be excluded and in particular, the British Rail Pocket Books will not be available at a discounted price. These books may still be ordered through the club, at the normal retail price.

THE PLATFORM 5
TRANSPORT BOOK CLUB
MEMBERSHIP APPLICATION FORM

To enrol for one year's membership in the PLATFORM 5 TRANSPORT BOOK CLUB, please complete this form (or a photocopy) and send it with your cheque/postal order for £1.50 made payable to 'Platform 5 Publishing Limited' to:

The Platform 5 Transport Book Club, Wyvern House, Old Forge Business Park, Sark Road, SHEFFIELD, S2 4HG.

BLOCK CAPITALS PLEASE

Name:. . . . .

Address:. . . . .

. . . .

Post Code:. . . . .

Please accept my application and enrol me as a member of the Platform 5 Transport Book Club.

As a member I will receive four issues of the club newsletter, each containing a number of new books at prices of at least 15% less than the published cover price (exclusive of postage and packing).

I understand I am not obliged to buy any of the books offered, and there is no limit to the number of copies of each book that may be ordered.

I enclose my cheque/postal order for £1.50 payable to Platform 5 Publishing Limited.

Signed: . . . .

Date: . . . .

Office Use Only:. . . . .

PLATFORM 5 PUBLISHING LTD.
MAIL ORDER LIST

NEW TITLES	Price
Motive Power Pocket Book Summer/Autumn 1993	1.80
Preserved Locomotives of British Railways 8th edition **JULY**	12.50
Diesel & Electric Loco Register 3rd edition **SEPTEMBER**	7.95
German Railways Locomotives & Multiple Units 3rd edition	12.50
Manx Electric **JULY**	8.95
Exeter-Newton Abbot – A Railway History **NOVEMBER**	25.00
Rambles by Rail 4: The New Forest	1.95
Bus Review 8 (Bus Enthusiast)	4.95

Modern British Railway Titles

British Railways Locomotives & Coaching Stock 1993	7.25
Coaching Stock Pocket Book 1993	1.80
Diesel Unit Pocket Book 1993	1.80
Electric Unit Pocket Book 1993	1.80
Departmental Coaching Stock 4th Edition	4.95
On-Track Plant on British Railways 4th Edition	5.50
The Fifty 50s in Colour	5.95
Today's Railways Review of the Year Volume 1	11.95
Today's Railways Review of the Year Volume 2	11.95
Today's Railways Review of the Year Volume 3	13.95
Today's Railways Review of the Year Volume 4	14.95
British Rail Internal Users (SCTP)	7.95
British Rail Wagon Fleet – Air Braked Stock (SCTP)	6.95
RIV Wagon Fleet (SCTP)	5.95
Miles & Chains Volume 2 – London Midland (Milepost)	1.40
Miles & Chains Vol. 3 – Scottish, Vol. 5 – Southern (Milepost)	each 1.00

Overseas Railways

Swiss Railways/Chemins de Fer Suisses	9.95
French Railways/Chemins de Fer Francais 2nd Edition	9.95
ÖBB/Austrian Federal Railways 2nd Edition	6.95
Benelux Locomotives & Coaching Stock 2nd Edition	6.95
A Guide to Portuguese Railways (Fearless)	4.95

Historical Railway Titles

6203 'Princess Margaret Rose'	19.95
Midland Railway Portrait	12.95
Steam Days on BR 1 – The Midland Line in Sheffield	4.95
Rails along the Sea Wall (Dawlish – Teignmouth Pictorial)	4.95
The Rolling Rivers	6.95
British Baltic Tanks	6.95
The Railways of Winchester	6.95
British Railways Mark 1 Coaches (Atlantic)	19.95
Register of Closed Railways 1948 – 91 (Milepost)	5.95
Private Owner Wagons Volume 3 (Headstock)	6.95
Private Owner Wagons Volume 4 (Headstock)	7.95

PVC Book Covers

A6 Pocket Book Covers in Blue, Red, Green or Grey	0.80
Locomotives & CS Covers in Blue, Red, Green or Grey	1.00
A5 Book Covers in Blue, Red, Green or Grey	1.40

Rambling	Price
Rambles by Rail 1 – The Hope Valley Line	1.95
Rambles by Rail 2 – Liskeard-Looe	1.95

Political

The Battle for the Settle & Carlisle	6.95

Light Rail Transit, Trams, Buses & Ships

Light Rail Review 1 (Reprint)	6.95
Light Rail Review 2	7.50
Light Rail Review 3	7.50
Light Rail Review 4	7.50
UK Light Rail Systems No.1: Manchester Metrolink	8.50
Blackpool & Fleetwood By Tram	7.50
London Buses in Exile 2nd Edition (Bus Enthusiast)	4.95
60 Years of A1 Service (Bus Enthusiast)	5.95
Edinburgh's Trams & Buses (Bus Enthusiast)	4.95
Speed Bonny Boat (The Story of Caledonian MacBrayne 1969-1990)	4.95

Maps & Track Diagrams (Quail Map Company)

British Rail Track Diagrams 1 – Scotland & Isle of Man	5.00
British Rail Track Diagrams 3 – Western	5.00
British Rail Track Diagrams 4 – London Midland	6.95
London Railway Map	5.95
London Transport Track Map	1.30
Czech Republic & Slovakia Railway Map	1.70
Greece Railway Map	1.00
Poland Railway Map	2.00
Hamburg Railway & Track Maps	1.00
Munich & Nuremberg U-Bahn Track Maps	0.60
New York Railway Map	1.70
Paris Railway Map	1.30

Back Numbers

Locomotives & Coaching Stock 1985	2.95
Locomotives & Coaching Stock 1986	3.30
Locomotives & Coaching Stock 1987	3.30
Locomotives & Coaching Stock 1988	3.95
Locomotives & Coaching Stock 1989	4.95
Locomotives & Coaching Stock 1990	5.95
Locomotives & Coaching Stock 1991	6.60
British Railways Locomotives & Coaching Stock 1992	7.00

Reduced Price Titles

The Handbook of British Railways Steam Motive Power Depots

Volume 1 – Southern England (was 7.95)	3.95
Volume 2 – Central England, East Anglia & Wales (was 8.95)	3.95
Volume 3 – North Midlands, Lancashire & Yorkshire (was 8.95)	3.95
Volume 4 – Northern England & Scotland (was 9.95)	3.95
North West Rails in Colour (was 8.50)	4.25
Along LMS Routes Vol. 1. (Headstock) (was 14.95)	6.95

Postage: 10% (UK), 20% (Overseas). Minimum 30p. Postage on reduced titles must be based on original price.

All these publications are available from shops, bookstalls or direct from: Mail Order Department, Platform 5 Publishing Ltd., Wyvern House, Old Forge Business Park, Sark Road, SHEFFIELD, S2 4HG, ENGLAND. For a full list of titles available by mail order, please send SAE to the above address.

56047	FC	NKJM	SL	
56048	FR	NKJM	SL	
56049	C	NKJM	SL	
56050	FA	FMTY	TE	
56051	FA	FASB	SL	
56052	FA	NKJM	SL	
56053	FA	FMCK	CF	Sir Morgannwg Ganol/ County of Mid Glamorgan
56054	FC	FMCK	CF	British Steel Llanwern
56055	FA	FASB	SL	
56056	FA	FASB	SL	
56057	FA	FASB	SL	
56058	FA	FASB	SL	
56059	FA	FASB	SL	
56060	FA	FMCK	CF	The Cardiff Rod Mill
56061	FM	FMTY	TE	
56062	FA	FCEN	TO	Mountsorrel
56063	FA	FMTY	TE	Bardon Hill
56064	FA	FMCK	CF	
56065	FA	FASB	SL	
56066	FC	FCXX	TO	
56067	FC	FCDN	TO	
56068	FC	FCDN	TO	
56069	§ FM	FMTY	TE	
56070	FA	FASB	SL	
56071	FC	FCDN	TO	
56072	FC	FCDN	TO	
56073	FM	FMCK	CF	Tremorfa Steelworks
56074	FC	FCDN	TO	Kellingley Colliery
56075	FC	FCDN	TO	West Yorkshire Enterprise
56076	FC	FMCK	CF	
56077	§ FC	FCDN	TO	Thorpe Marsh Power Station
56078	FA	FCDN	TO	
56079	FC	FCDN	TO	
56080	FC	FCDN	TO	Selby Coalfield
56081	FC	FCDN	TO	
56082	FC	FCDN	TO	
56083	* FC	FCDN	TO	
56084	* FC	FCDN	TO	
56085	FC	FCDN	TO	
56086	* FC	FCDN	TO	
56087	FM	FMTY	TE	
56088	FC	FCDN	TO	
56089	FC	FCDN	TO	Ferrybridge C Power Station
56090	FC	FCDN	TO	
56091	FC	FCDN	TO	Castle Donington Power Station
56092	FC	FCDN	TO	
56093	FC	FCDN	TO	The Institution of Mining Engineers
56094	FC	FCEN	TO	Eggborough Power Station
56095	FC	FCDN	TO	Harworth Colliery
56096	FC	FCDN	TO	

56097	FM	FMTY	TE	
56098	FC	FCDN	TO	
56099	FC	FCDN	TO	Fiddlers Ferry Power Station
56100	FC	FCDN	TO	
56101	FC	FCDN	TO	Mutual Improvement
56102	FC	FCEN	TO	Scunthorpe Steel Centenary
56103	FA	FASB	SL	
56104	FC	FCPA	TO	
56105	FA	FASB	SL	
56106	FC	FCEN	TO	
56107 §	FC	FCEN	TO	
56108	FR	FCEN	TO	
56109	FC	FCEN	TO	
56110	FA	FCEN	TO	Croft
56111	FC	FCEN	TO	
56112	FC	FCEN	TO	
56113	FC	FCKK	CF	
56114	FC	FCKK	CF	Maltby Colliery
56115	FC	FCKK	CF	
56116	FC	FMTY	TE	
56117	FC	FCEN	TO	Wilton-Coalpower
56118	FC	FCEN	TO	
56119	FC	FCKK	CF	
56120	FC	FCEN	TO	
56121	FC	FCPA	TO	
56123	FC	FCPA	TO	Drax Power Station
56124	BR	FCPA	TO	
56125	FC	FCPA	TO	
56126	BR	FCEN	TO	
56127	FC	FCPA	TO	
56128	FC	FCPA	TO	West Burton Power Station
56129	FC	FCPA	TO	
56130	FC	FCEN	TO	Wardley Opencast
56131	FC	FCEN	TO	Ellington Colliery
56132	FC	FCEN	TO	
56133	FC	FCEN	TO	Crewe Locomotive Works
56134	FC	FCEN	TO	Blyth Power
56135	FC	FCEN	TO	Port of Tyne Authority

CLASS 58   BREL TYPE 5   Co–Co

Built: 1983 – 87 by BREL at Doncaster Works.
Engine: Ruston Paxman RK3ACT of 2460 kW (3300 hp) at 1000 rpm.
Main Alternator: Brush BA1101B.
Traction Motors: Brush TM73-62.
Max. Tractive Effort: 275 kN (61800 lbf).
Cont. Tractive Effort: 240 kN (53950 lbf) at 17.4 mph.

Power At Rail: 1780 kW (2387 hp).	**Length over Buffers:** 19.13 m.
Brake Force: 62 t.	**Wheel Diameter:** 1120 mm.
Design Speed: 80 mph.	**Weight:** 130 t.
Max. Speed: 80 mph.	**RA:** 7.

Train Brakes: Air.
Multiple Working: Red Diamond coupling code.
Communication Equipment: Cab to shore radio-telephone.
All equipped with slow speed control.

58001	**FC**	FCBN	TO	
58002	**FC**	FCBN	TO	Daw Mill Colliery
58003	**FC**	FCBN	TO	Markham Colliery
58004	**FC**	FCBN	TO	
58005	**FC**	FCBN	TO	
58006	**FC**	FCBN	TO	
58007	**FC**	FCBN	TO	Drakelow Power Station
58008	**FC**	FCBN	TO	
58009	**FC**	FCBN	TO	
58010	**FC**	FCBN	TO	
58011	**FC**	FCBN	TO	
58012	**FC**	FCBN	TO	
58013	**FC**	FCBN	TO	
58014	**FC**	FCBN	TO	Didcot Power Station
58015	**FC**	FCBN	TO	
58016	**FC**	FCBN	TO	
58017	**FC**	FCBN	TO	
58018	**FC**	FCBN	TO	High Marnham Power Station
58019	**FC**	FCBN	TO	Shirebrook Colliery
58020	**FC**	FCBN	TO	Doncaster Works
58021	**FC**	FCBN	TO	
58022	**FC**	FCBN	TO	
58023	**FC**	FCBN	TO	
58024	**FC**	FCBN	TO	
58025	**FC**	FCBN	TO	
58026	**FC**	FCBN	TO	
58027	**FC**	FCBN	TO	
58028	**FC**	FCBN	TO	
58029	**FC**	FCBN	TO	
58030	**FC**	FCBN	TO	
58031	**FC**	FCBN	TO	
58032	**FC**	FCBN	TO	
58033	**FC**	FCBN	TO	
58034	**FC**	FCBN	TO	Bassetlaw
58035	**FC**	FCBN	TO	
58036	**FC**	FCBN	TO	
58037	**FC**	FCBN	TO	
58038	**FC**	FCBN	TO	
58039	**FC**	FCDN	TO	Rugeley Power Station
58040	**FC**	FCDN	TO	Cottam Power Station
58041	**FC**	FCBN	TO	Ratcliffe Power Station
58042	**FC**	FCDN	TO	Ironbridge Power Station
58043	**FC**	FCDN	TO	Knottingley
58044	**FC**	FCDN	TO	Oxcroft Opencast
58045	**FC**	FCDN	TO	
58046	**FC**	FCDN	TO	Thoresby Colliery

58047	**FC**	FCDN	TO	Manton Colliery
58048	**FC**	FCDN	TO	Coventry Colliery
58049	**FC**	FCDN	TO	Littleton Colliery
58050	**FC**	FCDN	TO	Toton Traction Depot

CLASS 59   GENERAL MOTORS TYPE 5   Co – Co

Built: 1985 (59001 – 4), 1989 (59005) by General Motors, La Grange, Illinois,
U.S.A. or 1990 (59101 – 4) by General Motors, London, Ontario, Canada.
Engine: General Motors 645E3C two stroke of 2460 kW (3300 hp) at 900 rpm.
Main Alternator: General Motors AR11 MLD-D14A.
Traction Motors: General Motors D77B.
Max. Tractive Effort: 506 kN (113 550 lbf).
Cont. Tractive Effort: 291 kN (65 300 lbf) at 14.3 mph.
Power At Rail: 1889 kW (2533 hp).   **Length over Buffers:** 21.35 m.
Brake Force: 69 t.   **Wheel Diameter:** 1067 mm.
Design Speed: 60 mph.   **Weight:** 121 t.
Max. Speed: 60 mph.   **RA:** 7.

Class 59/0. Owned by Foster-Yeoman Ltd. Blue/silver/blue livery with white lettering and cast numberplates.

59001	**0**	XYPO	FY	YEOMAN ENDEAVOUR
59002	**0**	XYPO	FY	YEOMAN ENTERPRISE
59003	**0**	XYPO	FY	YEOMAN HIGHLANDER
59004	**0**	XYPO	FY	YEOMAN CHALLENGER
59005	**0**	XYPO	FY	KENNETH J. PAINTER

Class 59/1. Owned by ARC Limited. Yellow/grey with grey lettering.

59101	**0**	XYPA	AR	Village of Whatley
59102	**0**	XYPA	AR	Village of Chantry
59103	**0**	XYPA	AR	Village of Mells
59104	**0**	XYPA	AR	Village of Great Elm

Class 59/2. Under construction for National Power.

| 59201 | **0** | | | |

CLASS 60   BRUSH TYPE 5   Co – Co

Built: 1989 onwards by Brush Traction.
Engine: Mirrlees MB275T of 2310 kW (3100 hp) at 1000 rpm.
Main Alternator: Brush .
Traction Motors: Brush separately excited.
Max. Tractive Effort: 500 kN (106500 lbf).
Cont. Tractive Effort: 336 kN (71570 lbf) at 17.4 mph.
Power At Rail: 1800 kW (2415 hp).   **Length over Buffers:** 21.34 m.
Brake Force: 74 t.   **Wheel Diameter:** 1118 mm.
Design Speed: 62 mph.   **Weight:** 129 t.
Max. Speed: 60 mph.   **RA:** 7.
Multiple Working: Within class.
Communication Equipment: Cab to shore radio-telephone.
All equipped with slow speed control.

60001	FA	FASB	SL	Steadfast
60002	FP	FPDI	IM	Capability Brown
60003	FP	FPDI	IM	Christopher Wren
60004	FC	FCJN	TO	Lochnagar
60005	FA	FABI	IM	Skiddaw
60006	FA	FAXN	TO	Great Gable
60007	FP	FPTY	TE	Robert Adam
60008	FM	FPDI	IM	Moel Fammau
60009	FA	FAXN	TO	Carnedd Dafydd
60010	FA	FAXN	TO	Pumlumon Plynlimon
60011	FA	FAXN	TO	Cader Idris
60012	FA	FAXN	TO	Glyder Fawr
60013	FP	FPDI	IM	Robert Boyle
60014	FP	FPDI	IM	Alexander Fleming
60015	FA	FABI	IM	Bow Fell
60016	FA	FABI	IM	Langdale Pikes
60017	FA	FASB	SL	Arenig Fawr
60018	FA	FASB	SL	Moel Siabod
60019	FA	FASB	SL	Wild Boar Fell
60020	FM	FMMY	TE	Great Whernside
60021	FM	FPDI	IM	Pen-y-Ghent
60022	FM	FMMY	TE	Ingleborough
60023	FM	FMMY	TE	The Cheviot
60024	FP	FPDI	IM	Elizabeth Fry
60025	FP	FPDI	IM	Joseph Lister
60026	FP	FPDI	IM	William Caxton
60027	FP	FPDI	IM	Joseph Banks
60028	FP	FPDI	IM	John Flamsteed
60029	FM	FMEK	CF	Ben Nevis
60030	FM	FMMY	TE	Cir Mhor
60031	FM	FMMY	TE	Ben Lui
60032	FC	FCHN	TO	William Booth
60033	FP	FPEK	CF	Anthony Ashley Cooper
60034	FM	FMEK	CF	Carnedd Llewelyn
60035	FM	FMEK	CF	Florence Nightingale
60036	FM	FMEK	CF	Sgurr Na Ciche
60037	FM	FMEK	CF	Helvellyn
60038	FM	FMMY	TE	Bidean Nam Bian
60039	FA	FASB	SL	Glastonbury Tor
60040	FA	FASB	SL	Brecon Beacons
60041	FA	FASB	SL	High Willhays
60042	FA	FASB	SL	Dunkery Beacon
60043	FA	FASB	SL	Yes Tor
60044	FM	FCHN	TO	Ailsa Craig
60045	FC	FCHN	TO	Josephine Butler
60046	FC	FCHN	TO	William Wilberforce
60047	FC	FCHN	TO	Robert Owen
60048	FA	FAXN	TO	Saddleback
60049	FM	FMMY	TE	Scafell
60050	FM	FPDI	IM	Roseberry Topping
60051	FP	FPEK	CF	Mary Somerville

60052	FM	FMMY	TE	Goat Fell
60053	FP	FPDI	IM	John Reith
60054	FP	FPDI	IM	Charles Babbage
60055	FC	FCHN	TO	Thomas Barnardo
60056	FC	FCHN	TO	William Beveridge
60057	FC	FCHN	TO	Adam Smith
60058	FC	FCHN	TO	John Howard
60059	FC	FCJN	TO	Samuel Plimsoll
60060	FC	FCHN	TO	James Watt
60061	FC	FCHN	TO	Alexander Graham Bell
60062	FP	FPEK	CF	Samuel Johnson
60063	FP	FPEK	CF	James Murray
60064	FP	FPDI	IM	Back Tor
60065	FP	FPEK	CF	Kinder Low
60066	FC	FCHN	TO	John Logie Baird
60067	FC	FCJN	TO	James Clerk-Maxwell
60068	FC	FCJN	TO	Charles Darwin
60069	FC	FCJN	TO	Humphry Davy
60070	FC	FCJN	TO	John Loudon McAdam
60071	FC	FCJN	TO	Dorothy Garrod
60072	FC	FCJN	TO	Cairn Toul
60073	FC	FCJN	TO	Cairn Gorm
60074	FC	FCJN	TO	Braeriach
60075	FC	FCJN	TO	Liathach
60076	FC	FCJN	TO	Suilven
60077	FC	FCJN	TO	Canisp
60078	FC	FCJN	TO	Stac Pollaidh
60079	FC	FCJN	TO	Foinaven
60080	FA	FABI	IM	Kinder Scout
60081	FA	FMEK	CF	Bleaklow Hill
60082	FA	FABI	IM	Mam Tor
60083	FA	FAXN	TO	Shining Tor
60084	FA	FABI	IM	Cross Fell
60085	FA	FABI	IM	Axe Edge
60086	FC	FCJN	TO	Schiehallion
60087	FC	FCJN	TO	Slioch
60088	FC	FCJN	TO	Buachaille Etive Mor
60089	FC	FCJN	TO	Arcuil
60090	FC	FPTY	TE	Quinag
60091	FC	FPDI	IM	An Teallach
60092	FC	FPEK	CF	Reginald Munns
60093	FC	FMEK	CF	Jack Stirk
60094	FA	FAXN	TO	Tryfan
60095	FA	FABI	IM	Crib Goch
60096	FA	FMEK	CF	Ben Macdui
60097	FA	FABI	IM	Pillar
60098	FA	FAXN	TO	Charles Francis Brush
60099	FA	FAXN	TO	Ben More Assynt
60100	FA	FAXN	TO	Boar of Badenoch

BR ELECTRIC LOCOMOTIVES

CLASS 73/0   ELECTRO – DIESEL   Bo – Bo

Built: 1962 by BR at Eastleigh Works.
Supply System: 660 – 850 V d.c. from third rail.
Engine: English Electric 4SRKT of 447 kW (600 hp) at 850 rpm.
Main Generator: English Electric 824/3D.
Traction Motors: English Electric 542A.
Max. Tractive Effort: Electric 187 kN (42000 lbf). Diesel 152 kN (34100 lbf).
Continuous Rating: Electric 1060 kW (1420 hp) giving a tractive effort of 43 kN (9600 lbf) at 55.5 mph.
Cont. Tractive Effort: Diesel 72 kN (16100 lbf) at 10 mph.
Maximum Rail Power: Electric 1830 kW (2450 hp) at 37 mph.

Brake Force: 31 t.	**Length over Buffers:** 16.36 m.
Design Speed: 80 mph.	**Weight:** 76.5 t.
Max. Speed: 60 mph.	**RA:** 6.
Wheel Diameter: 1016 mm.	**ETH Index (Elec. power):** 66

Train Brakes: Air, Vacuum and electro-pneumatic.
Multiple Working: Within sub-class, with Class 33/1 and various SR EMUs.
Communication Equipment: All equipped with driver – guard telephone.
Couplings: Drop-head buckeye.
Formerly numbered E 6001 – /3/5/6.

Non-standard Livery: 73005 is Network SouthEast blue.

73001		RCRB	BD
73002	**BR**	RCRB	BD
73003	**G**	NXXA	SL (S) Sir Herbert Walker
73005	**0**	RCRB	BD Mid Hants WATERCRESS LINE
73006	**BR**	RCRB	BD

CLASS 73/1 & 73/2   ELECTRO – DIESEL   Bo – Bo

Built: 1965 – 67 by English Electric Co. at Vulcan Foundry, Newton le Willows.
Engine: English Electric 4SRKT of 447 kW (600 hp) at 850 rpm.
Main Generator: English Electric 824/5D.
Traction Motors: English Electric 546/1B.
Supply System: 660 – 850 V d.c. from third rail.
Max. Tractive Effort: Electric 179 kN (40000 lbf). Diesel 160 kN (36000 lbf).
Continuous Rating: Electric 1060 kW (1420 hp) giving a tractive effort of 35 kN (7800 lbf) at 68 mph.
Cont. Tractive Effort: Diesel 60 kN (13600 lbf) at 11.5 mph.
Maximum Rail Power: Electric 2350 kW (3150 hp) at 42 mph.

Brake Force: 31 t.	**Length over Buffers:** 16.36 m.
Design Speed: 90 mph.	**Weight:** 77 t.
Max. Speed: 60 (90*) mph.	**RA:** 6.
Wheel Diameter: 1016 mm.	**ETH Index (Elec. power):** 66

Train Brakes: Air, Vacuum and electro-pneumatic.
Multiple Working: Within sub-class, with Class 33/1 and various SR EMUs.

Communication Equipment: All equipped with driver – guard telephone.
Couplings: Drop-head buckeye.
Non-standard Livery: 73101 is Pullman umber & Cream.

Class 73/2 are locos dedicated to InterCity and Network SouthEast services.

a Vacuum brake isolated.

Formerly numbered E 6001 – 20/22 – 26/28 – 49 (not in order).

73101		**0**	NKJL	SL	The Royal Alex'
73103		**I0**	NKJL	SL	
73104		**I0**	NKJL	SL	
73105		**C**	NKJL	SL	
73106		**D**	NKJL	SL	
73107		**C**	NKJL	SL	
73108		**C**	NKJL	SL	
73109	*	**N**	NWXB	BM	Battle of Britain 50th Anniversary
73110		**C**	NKJL	SL	
73114		**I0**	NKJR	SL	
73117		**I0**	NKJL	SL	University of Surrey
73118		**C**	NKJL	SL	The Romney Hythe and Dymchurch Railway
73119		**C**	NKJL	SL	Kentish Mercury
73126		**N**	NKJR	SL	Kent & East Sussex Railway
73128		**C**	NKJR	SL	OVS BULLIED C.B.E. 1937 1949 C.M.E. SOUTHERN RAILWAY
73129		**N**	NKJL	SL	City of Winchester
73130		**C**	NKJL	SL	City of Portsmouth
73131		**C**	NKJR	SL	County of Surrey
73132		**I0**	NKJR	SL	
73133		**N**	NKJL	SL	The Bluebell Railway
73134		**I0**	NKJR	SL	Woking Homes 1885 – 1985
73136		**N**	NKJL	SL	Kent Youth Music
73138		**C**	NKJL	SL	
73139		**I0**	NKJR	SL	
73140		**I0**	NKJR	SL	
73141		**I0**	NKJR	SL	
73201 (73142)	a*	**I**	IVGA	SL	Broadlands
73202 (73137)	*	**I**	IVGA	SL	Royal Observer Corps
73203 (73127)	a*	**I**	IVGA	SL	
73204 (73125)	a*	**I**	IVGA	SL	Stewarts Lane 1860 – 1985
73205 (73124)	*	**M**	IVGA	SL	London Chamber of Commerce
73206 (73123)	a*	**I**	IVGA	SL	Gatwick Express
73207 (73122)	a*	**I**	IVGA	SL	County of East Sussex
73208 (73121)	a*	**I**	IVGA	SL	Croydon 1883 – 1983
73209 (73120)	a*	**I**	IVGA	SL	
73210 (73116)	a*	**I**	IVGA	SL	Selhurst
73211 (73113)	a*	**I**	IVGA	SL	
73212 (73102)	*	**I**	IVGA	SL	Airtour Suisse
73235 (73135)	a*	**I**	IVGA	SL	

NOTES FOR CLASSES 86–91.

The following common features apply to all locos of Classes 86–91.
Supply System: 25 kV a.c. from overhead equipment.
Communication Equipment: Driver – guard telephone and cab to shore radio-telephone.
Multiple Working: Time division multiplex system.

CLASS 86/1   BR DESIGN   Bo–Bo

Built: 1965 – 66 by English Electric Co. at Vulcan Foundry, Newton le Willows or BR at Doncaster Works. Rebuilt with Class 87 type bogies and motors. Tap changer control.
Traction Motors: GEC G412AZ frame mounted.
Max. Tractive Effort: 258 kN (58000 lbf).
Continuous Rating: 3730 kW (5000 hp) giving a tractive effort of 95 kN (21300 lbf) at 87 mph.
Maximum Rail Power: 5860 kW (7860 hp) at ?? mph.

Brake Force: 40 t.	**Length over Buffers:** 17.83 m.
Design Speed: 110 mph.	**Weight:** 87 t.
Max. Speed: 110 mph.	**RA:** 6.
ETH Index: 74	**Wheel Diameter:** 1150 mm.
Train Brakes: Air & Vacuum.	**Electric Brake:** Rheostatic.

Note: Class 86 were formerly numbered E 3101 – 3200 (not in order).

86101	(86201)	M	IWPA	WN	Sir William A Stanier FRS
86102	(86202)	I0	IWPA	WN	Robert A Riddles
86103	(86203)	I	IWPA	WN	André Chapelon

CLASS 86/2   BR DESIGN   Bo–Bo

Built: 1965 – 66 by English Electric Co. at Vulcan Foundry, Newton le Willows or BR at Doncaster Works. Later rebuilt with resilient wheels and flexicoil suspension. Tap changer control.
Traction Motors: AEI 282BZ.
Max. Tractive Effort: 207 kN (46500 lbf).
Continuous Rating: 3010 kW (4040 hp) giving a tractive effort of 85 kN (19200 lbf) at 77.5 mph.
Maximum Rail Power: 4550 kW (6100 hp) at 49.5 mph.

Brake Force: 40 t.	**Length over Buffers:** 17.83 m.
Design Speed: 125 mph.	**Weight:** 85 t – 86 t.
Max. Speed: 100 (110§) mph.	**RA:** 6.
ETH Index: 74	**Wheel Diameter:** 1156 mm.
Train Brakes: Air & Vacuum.	**Electric Brake:** Rheostatic.

86204		I	IWPA	WN	City of Carlisle
86205	(86503)	I	ICCA	LG	City of Lancaster
86206		M	ICCA	LG	City of Stoke on Trent
86207		I	IWPA	WN	City of Lichfield
86208		I	IWPA	WN	City of Chester
86209		§ M	IWPA	WN	City of Coventry

86210		I	IWPA	WN	City of Edinburgh
86212		M	ICCA	LG	Preston Guild 1328 – 1992
86213		I	IWPA	WN	Lancashire Witch
86214		I	ICCA	LG	Sans Pareil
86215		M	IANA	NC	Joseph Chamberlain
86216		I	ICCA	LG	Meteor
86217	(86504)	I	IANA	NC	Halley's Comet
86218		I	IANA	NC	Harold MacMillan
86219		I	IWPA	WN	Phoenix
86220		I	IANA	NC	The Round Tabler
86221		M	IANA	NC	B.B.C. Look East
86222	(86502)	I	ICCA	LG	LLOYD'S LIST
					250th ANNIVERSARY
86223		I	IANA	NC	Norwich Union
86224		§ I	IWPA	WN	Caledonian
86225		§ I	IWPA	WN	Hardwicke
86226		M	ICCA	LG	Royal Mail Midlands
86227		M	ICCA	LG	Sir Henry Johnson
86228		I	ICCA	LG	Vulcan Heritage
86229		I	ICCA	LG	Sir John Betjeman
86230		M	IANA	NC	The Duke of Wellington
86231		§ I	IWPA	WN	Starlight Express
86232		I	IANA	NC	Norwich Festival
86233	(86506)	I	ICCA	LG	Laurence Olivier
86234		I	ICCA	LG	J B Priestley OM
86235		I	IANA	NC	Crown Point
86236		I	IWPA	WN	Josiah Wedgwood
					MASTER POTTER 1736 – 1795
86237		I	IANA	NC	Sir Charles Hallé
86238		I	IANA	NC	European Community
86239	(86507)	R	PXLE	CE	L S Lowry
86240		I	IWPA	WN	Bishop Eric Treacy
86241	(86508)	R	PXLE	CE	Glenfiddich
86242		M	IWPA	WN	James Kennedy GC
86243		IO	PXLE	CE	The Boys' Brigade
86244		I	ICCA	LG	The Royal British Legion
86245		I	IWPA	WN	Dudley Castle
86246	(86505)	I	IANA	NC	Royal Anglian Regiment
86247		I	ICCA	LG	Abraham Darby
86248		I	IWPA	WN	Sir Clwyd/County of Clwyd
86249		M	IANA	NC	County of Merseyside
86250		I	IANA	NC	The Glasgow Herald
86251		M	IWPA	WN	The Birmingham Post
86252		IO	ICCA	LG	The Liverpool Daily Post
86253	(86044)	I	IWPA	WN	The Manchester Guardian
86254	(86047)	RX	PXLE	CE	
86255	(86042)	I	ICCA	LG	Penrith Beacon
86256	(86040)	M	IWPA	WN	
86257	(86043)	I	IWPA	WN	Snowdon
86258	(86501)	I	IWPA	WN	Talyllyn – The First Preserved
					Railway

86259 (86045)	**I**	ICCA	LG	Peter Pan
86260 (86048)	**I**	ICCA	LG	Driver Wallace Oakes G.C.
86261 (86041)	**RX**	PXLE	CE	

CLASS 86/4 & 86/6   BR DESIGN   Bo – Bo

Built: 1965 – 66 by English Electric Co. at Vulcan Foundry, Newton le Willows or BR at Doncaster Works. Later rebuilt with resilient wheels and flexicoil suspension. Tap changer control.
Traction Motors: AEI 282AZ.
Max. Tractive Effort: 258 kN (58000 lbf).
Continuous Rating: 2680 kW (3600 hp) giving a tractive effort of 89 kN (20000 lbf) at 67 mph.
Maximum Rail Power: 4400 kW (5900 hp) at 38 mph.

Brake Force: 40 t.	**Length over Buffers:** 17.83 m.
Design Speed: 100 mph.	**Weight:** 83 t – 84 t.
Max. Speed: 100 (75*) mph.	**RA:** 6.
ETH Index: 74	**Wheel Diameter:** 1156 mm.
Train Brakes: Air & Vacuum.	**Electric Brake:** Rheostatic.

Class 86/6 have the ETH equipment isolated.

Note: 86405/11/4/5/28/31 have recently been renumbered from 86/6.

86401 (86001)	**RX**	PXLE	CE	
86602 (86402)	* **FD**	MDNC	CE	
86603 (86403)	* **FD**	MDNC	CE	
86604 (86404)	* **FD**	MDNC	CE	
86405 (86605)	**FD**	PXLE	CE	Intercontainer
86606 (86406)	* **FD**	MDNC	CE	
86607 (86407)	* **FD**	MDNC	CE	The Institution of Electrical Engineers
86608 (86408)	* **FD**	MDNC	CE	St. John Ambulance
86609 (86409)	* **FD**	MDNC	CE	
86610 (86410)	* **FD**	MDNC	CE	
86411 (86611)	**FD**	PXLE	CE	Airey Neave
86612 (86412)	* **FD**	MDNC	CE	Elizabeth Garrett Anderson
86613 (86413)	* **FD**	MDNC	CE	County of Lancashire
86414 (86614)	**FD**	PXLE	CE	Frank Hornby
86415 (86615)	**FD**	PXLE	CE	Rotary International
86416 (86316)	**RX**	PXLE	CE	
86417 (86317)	**RX**	PXLE	CE	
86618 (86418)	* **FD**	MDNC	CE	
86419 (86319)	**R**	PXLE	CE	Post Haste 150 YEARS OF TRAVELLING POST OFFICES
86620 (86420)	* **FD**	MDNC	CE	
86621 (86421)	* **FD**	MDNC	CE	London School of Economics
86622 (86422)	* **FD**	MDNC	CE	
86623 (86423)	* **FD**	MDNC	CE	
86424 (86324)	**R**	PXLE	CE	
86425 (86325)	**R**	PXLE	CE	
86426 (86326)	**RX**	PXLE	CE	

86627	(86427)	* FD MDNC	CE	The Industrial Society
86428	(86628)	FD PXLE	CE	Aldaniti
86430	(86030)	RX PXLE	CE	
86431	(86631)	FD PXLE	CE	
86632	(86432)	* FD MDNC	CE	Brookside
86633	(86433)	* FD MDNC	CE	Wulfruna
86634	(86434)	* FD MDNC	CE	University of London
86635	(86435)	* FD MDNC	CE	
86636	(86436)	* FD MDNC	CE	
86637	(86437)	* FD MDNC	CE	
86638	(86438)	* FD MDNC	CE	
86639	(86439)	* FD MDNC	CE	

CLASS 87   BR DESIGN   Bo – Bo

Built: 1973 – 75 by BREL at Crewe Works. Class 87/1 has thyristor control instead of HT tap changing.
Traction Motors: GEC G412AZ frame mounted (87/0), G412BZ (87/1).
Max. Tractive Effort: 258 kN (58000 lbf).
Continuous Rating: 3730 kW (5000 hp) giving a tractive effort of 95 kN (21300 lbf) at 87 mph (Class 87/0), 3620 kW (4850 hp) giving a tractive effort of 96 kN (21600 lbf) at 84 mph (Class 87/1).
Maximum Rail Power: 5860 kW (7860 hp) at ?? mph.
Brake Force: 40 t.
Design Speed: 110 mph
Max. Speed: 110 (75*) mph.
ETH Index: 95
Train Brakes: Air.
Length over Buffers: 17.83 m.
Weight: 83.5 t.
RA: 6.
Wheel Diameter: 1150 mm.
Electric Brake: Rheostatic.

Class 87/0. Standard Design. Tap Changer Control.

87001	I	IWSA	WN	Royal Scot
87002	I	IWSA	WN	Royal Sovereign
87003	I	IWSA	WN	Patriot
87004	I	IWSA	WN	Britannia
87005	I	IWSA	WN	City of London
87006	I0	IWSA	WN	City of Glasgow
87007	I	IWSA	WN	City of Manchester
87008	I	IWSA	WN	City of Liverpool
87009	I	IWSA	WN	City of Birmingham
87010	I	IWCA	WN	King Arthur
87011	M	IWCA	WN	The Black Prince
87012	M	IWCA	WN	The Royal Bank of Scotland
87013	I	IWCA	WN	John O' Gaunt
87014	I	IWCA	WN	Knight of the Thistle
87015	I	IWCA	WN	Howard of Effingham
87016	I	IWCA	WN	Willesden Intercity Depot
87017	I0	IWCA	WN	Iron Duke
87018	M	IWCA	WN	Lord Nelson
87019	I0	IWCA	WN	Sir Winston Churchill
87020	I0	IWCA	WN	North Briton
87021	I0	IWCA	WN	Robert the Bruce

87022	**M**	IWCA	WN	Cock o' the North
87023	**I0**	IWCA	WN	Velocity
87024	**I0**	IWCA	WN	Lord of the Isles
87025	**I0**	IWCA	WN	County of Cheshire
87026	**I0**	IWCA	WN	Sir Richard Arkwright
87027	**I0**	IWCA	WN	Wolf of Badenoch
87028	**M**	IWCA	WN	Lord President
87029	**I0**	IWCA	WN	Earl Marischal
87030	**I0**	IWCA	WN	Black Douglas
87031	**M**	IWCA	WN	Hal o' the Wynd
87032	**I0**	IWCA	WN	Kenilworth
87033	**M**	IWCA	WN	Thane of Fife
87034	**I0**	IWCA	WN	William Shakespeare
87035	**M**	IWCA	WN	Robert Burns

Class 87/1. Thyristor Control.

| 87101 | * | **FD** MDNC | CE | STEPHENSON |

CLASS 90   GEC DESIGN   Bo – Bo

Built: 1987 – 90 by BREL at Crewe Works. Thyristor control.
Traction Motors: GEC G412CY separately excited frame mounted.
Max. Tractive Effort: 192 kN (43150 lbf).
Continuous Rating: 3730 kW (5000 hp) giving a tractive effort of 95 kN (21300 lbf) at 87 mph.
Maximum Rail Power: 5860 kW (7860 hp) at ?? mph.

Brake Force: 40 t.	**Length over Buffers:** 18.80 m.
Design Speed: 110 mph.	**Weight:** 84.5 t.
Max. Speed: 110 (75*) mph.	**RA:** 7.
ETH Index: 95	**Wheel Diameter:** 1156 mm.
Train Brakes: Air.	**Electric Brake:** Rheostatic.
Couplings: Drop-head buckeye.	

Non-standard Liveries:

90128 is in SNCB/NMBS (Belgian Railways) electric loco livery.
90129 is in DB (German Federal Railways) 'neurot' livery.
90130 is in SNCF (French Railways) 'Sybic' livery.
90136 is in livery "FD", but with yellow ends and roof.

Class 90/0. As built.

90001	**I**	IWCA	WN	BBC Midlands Today
90002	**I**	IWCA	WN	The Girls' Brigade
90003	**I**	IWCA	WN	
90004	**I**	IWCA	WN	T D' Oyly Carte Opera Company
90005	**I**	IWCA	WN	Financial Times
90006	**I**	IWCA	WN	High Sheriff
90007	**I**	IWCA	WN	Lord Stamp
90008	**I**	IWCA	WN	The Birmingham Royal Ballet
90009	**I**	IWCA	WN	Royal Show
90010	**I**	IWCA	WN	275 Railway Squadron (Volunteers)
90011	**I**	IWCA	WN	The Chartered Institute of Transport

90012	I	IWCA	WN	Glasgow 1990 Cultural Capital
				of Europe
90013	I	IWCA	WN	The Law Society
90014	I	IWCA	WN	The Liverpool Phil
90015	I	IWCA	WN	BBC North West
90016	RX	PXLA	CE	
90017	RX	PXLA	CE	
90018	RX	PXLA	CE	
90019	RX	PXLA	CE	Penny Black
90020	RX	PXLA	CE	Colonel Bill Cockburn CBE TD
90021	FD	PXLA	CE	
90022	FD	MDLC	CE	Freightconnection
90023	FD	MDLC	CE	
90024	FD	MDLC	CE	
90025	FD	MDLC	CE	

Class 90/1. ETH equipment isolated. Renumbered from 90026 – 90150.

90126	*	FD	MDMC	CE	Crewe Electric Depot Quality Approved
90127	*	FD	MDMC	CE	Allerton T&RS Depot Quality Approved
90128	*	0	MDMC	CE	Vrachtverbinding
90129	*	0	MDMC	CE	Frachtverbindungen
90130	*	0	MDMC	CE	Fretconnection
90131	*	M	MDMC	CE	
90132	*	M	MDMC	CE	
90133	*	M	MDMC	CE	
90134	*	M	MDMC	CE	
90135	*	M	MDMC	CE	
90136	*	0	MDMC	CE	
90137	*	FD	MDMC	CE	
90138	*	FD	MDMC	CE	
90139	*	FD	MDMC	CE	
90140	*	FD	MDMC	CE	
90141	*	FD	MDMC	CE	
90142	*	FD	MDMC	CE	
90143	*	FD	MDMC	CE	
90144	*	FD	MDMC	CE	
90145	*	FD	MDMC	CE	
90146	*	FD	MDMC	CE	
90147	*	FD	MDMC	CE	
90148	*	FD	MDMC	CE	
90149	*	FD	MDMC	CE	
90150	*	FD	MDMC	CE	

CLASS 91   GEC DESIGN   Bo – Bo

Built: 1988 onwards by BREL at Crewe Works. Thyristor control.
Traction Motors: GEC G426AZ.
Continuous Rating: 4540 kW (6090 hp).
Maximum Rail Power: 4700 kW (6300 hp).
Brake Force: 45 t.   **Length over Buffers:** 19.40 m.
Design Speed: 140 mph.   **Weight:** 84 t.

Max. Speed: 140 mph.   **RA:** 7.
ETH Index: 95   **Wheel Diameter:** 1000 mm.
Train Brakes: Air.   **Electric Brake:** Rheostatic.
Couplings: Drop-head buckeye.

91001	I	IECA	BN	Swallow
91002	I	IECA	BN	
91003	I	IECA	BN	THE SCOTSMAN
91004	I	IECA	BN	The Red Arrows
91005	I	IECA	BN	Royal Air Force Regiment
91006	I	IECA	BN	
91007	I	IECA	BN	Ian Allan
91008	I	IECA	BN	Thomas Cook
91009	I	IECA	BN	Saint Nicholas
91010	I	IECA	BN	
91011	I	IECA	BN	Terence Cuneo
91012	I	IECA	BN	
91013	I	IECA	BN	Michael Faraday
91014	I	IECA	BN	Northern Electric
91015	I	IECA	BN	
91016	I	IECA	BN	
91017	I	IECA	BN	
91018	I	IECA	BN	
91019	I	IECA	BN	Scottish Enterprise
91020	I	IECA	BN	
91021	I	IECA	BN	
91022	I	IECA	BN	
91023	I	IECA	BN	
91024	I	IECA	BN	
91025	I	IECA	BN	BBC Radio One FM
91026	I	IECA	BN	
91027	I	IECA	BN	
91028	I	IECA	BN	Guide Dog
91029	I	IECA	BN	Queen Elizabeth II
91030	I	IECA	BN	Palace of Holyroodhouse
91031	I	IECA	BN	Sir Henry Royce

CLASS 92   BRUSH DESIGN   Co–Co

Built: 1993 onwards by Brush Traction. Thyristor control.
Supply System: 25 kV a.c. from overhead equipment and 750 V d.c. third rail.
Electrical equipment: ABB Transportation, Zürich, Switzerland.
Traction Motors: Brush.
Max. Tractive Effort: 400 kN (90 000 lbf).
Continuous Rating at Motor Shaft: 5040 kW (6760 hp).
Maximum Rail Power: 5000 kW (6700 hp).
Brake Force: t.   **Length over Buffers:** 21.34 m.
Design Speed: 140 mph.   **Weight:** 126 t.
Max. Speed: 140 km/h (87.5 mph).   **RA:** .
ETH Index: **Wheel Diameter:** 1160 mm.
Train Brakes: Air.   **Electric Brake:** Rheostatic.

Couplings: Drop-head buckeye.
Multiple Working: Time division multiplex system.
Communication Equipment: Driver – guard telephone and cab to shore radio-telephone.
Cab Signalling: Fitted with TVM430 cab signalling for Channel Tunnel.

92001
92002
92003
92004
92005
92006
92007
92008
92009
92010
92011
92012
92013
92014
92015
92016
92017
92018
92019
92020
92021
92022
92023
92024
92025
92026
92027
92028
92029
92030
92031
92032
92033
92034
92035
92036
92037

BR DEPARTMENTAL LOCOMOTIVES

CLASS 97/2   BR TYPE 2   Bo – Bo

Built: 1966 by Beyer Peacock, Manchester (97251), BR at Derby Loco Works (97252). Converted to ETH generator vehicles (non self-propelled) to work with steam locomotives.
Engine: Sulzer 6LDA28-B of 930 kW (1250 hp) at 750 rpm.
Main Generator: AEI RTB 15656.
Brake Force: 38 t.   **Length over Buffers:** 15.39 m.
Weight: 71.7 t.   **Wheel Diameters:** 1143 mm.
Max. Speed: 90 mph.   **RA:** 5.
ETH Index: 66.

97251 (25305)	**M**	RAIL	IS
97252 (25314)	**M**	RAIL	IS

CLASS 97/6   RUSTON SHUNTER   0 – 6 – 0

Built: 1959 by Ruston & Hornsby at Lincoln.
Engine: Ruston 6VPH of 123 kW (165 hp).
Main Generator: British Thomson Houston RTB6034.
Traction Motor: One British Thomson Houston RTA5041.
Max. Tractive Effort: 75 kN (17000 lbf).
Brake Force: 16 t.   **Length over Buffers:** 7.62 m.
Weight: 31 t.   **Wheel Diameter:** 978 mm.
Max. Speed: 20 mph.   **RA:** 1.
Train Brakes: Vacuum.

Non-Standard Livery: Departmental Yellow.

97651 (PWM 651)	v	**0**	REJK	CF
97654 (PWM 654)	v	**0**	IGJK	RG

CLASS 97/7   BATTERY LOCOS   Bo – Bo

Built: 1973 – 80 by BREL at Doncaster and Wolverton Works. Converted from Class 501 EMU cars.
Supply System: 750 V d.c. third rail or 320 V d.c. batteries.
Traction Motors: GEC WT344A.
Max. Tractive Effort: 73 kN (16400 lbf).
Brake Force: 45 t.   **Length over Buffers:** 18.44 m.
Weight: 59 t.   **Wheel Diameter:** 1071 mm.
Max. Speed: 25 mph.   **RA:** 4.
Multiple Working: Work in pairs.
Non-Standard Livery: Bright blue with yellow stripe.

97701	(61136)	a	**0**	RCRB	BD
97702	(61139)	a	**0**	RCRB	BD
97703	(61182)	a		NKFH	HE
97704	(61185)	a		NKFH	HE

```
97705 (61184) a      NKFH   HE
97706 (61189) a      NKFH   HE
97707 (61166) a  N   NKFH   HE
97708 (61173) a  N   NKFH   HE
97709 (61172) a      NKFH   HE (S)
97710 (61175) a      NKFH   HE (S)
```

Note: 97701/2 carry DB 977363/2 in error.

CLASS 97/8   EE SHUNTER   0 – 6 – 0

For details see Class 09. Severn Tunnel emergency train locomotive.

Non-Standard Livery: BR blue with grey cab.

97806   (09017) xo   **0** IGJK   CF   Normally kept at Sudbrook.

DB 968xxx SERIES

This number series was introduced in 1969 and is for former capital stock locomotives which no longer operate under their own power.

Non-standard Livery: 968021 is British Rail Research red/blue/white.

```
ADB 968021   (84009) x  CE        Mobile load bank.
TDB 968030   (33018) x            Moreton-in-Marsh training loco.
```

EUROTUNNEL LOCOMOTIVES

CLASS 0   MaK   Bo – Bo

These general purpose diesel locomotives are the same basic design as the
Netherlands Railways 6400 Class.
Built: 1992 – 3 by Krupp-MaK/ABB at Kiel, Germany. (Type DE1004)
Engine: MaK 940 kW (1280 hp) at 1800 r.p.m.
Traction Motor: Four ABB three-phase traction motors.
Max. Tractive Effort: 305 kN.
Continuous Tractive Effort: 140 kN at 20 m.p.h.
Power at Rail: 750 kW.
Brake Force: 120 kN.   **Length over Buffers:** 15.90 m.
Weight: 84 tonnes   **Wheel Diameter:** 1000 mm.
Max. Speed: 60 mph.   **Train Brakes:** Air.
Communication Equipment: Cab to shore radio.
Couplings: High and Low level Sharfenberg plus UIC screw.
Cab Signalling: TVM 430.
Livery: Standard NS grey and yellow (Netherlands Railways).

0001	CQ
0002	CQ
0003	CQ
0004	CQ
0005	CQ

CLASS 9   BRUSH EUROSHUTTLE   Bo – Bo – Bo

A.C. electric locomotives which will be used on the Eurotunnel shuttle trains
between Cheriton and Coquelles.
Built: 1992 – 3 by Brush/ABB at Loughborough.
Supply System: 25 kV a.c. from overhead equipment.
Traction Motors:
Max. Tractive Effort: 400 kN (90 000 lbf).
Continuous Rating: 5760 kW (7725 hp) giving a tractive effort of 310 kN at
65 km/h.
Brake Force: 50 t.   **Length over Buffers:** 22.00 m.
Design Speed: 110 mph.   **Weight:** 132 t.
Max. Speed: 160 km/h (100 mph).   **RA:** Channel Tunnel only.
ETH Index: **Wheel Diameter:** 1090 mm.
Train Brakes: Air.   **Electric Brake:** Regenerative.
Multiple Working: Time division multiplex system.
Couplings: High and Low level Sharfenburg plus UIC screw.
Communication Equipment: Cab to shore radio.
Cab Signalling: TVM 430.
Livery: Metallic silver.

9001	CQ
9002	CQ
9003	
9004	
9005	
9006	
9007	
9008	
9009	
9010	
9011	
9012	
9013	
9014	
9015	
9016	
9017	
9018	
9019	
9020	
9021	
9022	
9023	
9024	
9025	
9026	
9027	
9028	
9029	
9030	
9031	
9032	
9033	
9034	
9035	
9036	
9037	
9038	

BR LOCOMOTIVES AWAITING DISPOSAL

03179**N**	Ryde T&RSMD	08656	Bletchley TMD
08222	Bounds Green T&RSMD	08657	York
08224	Doncaster TMD	08658	Norwich T&RSMD
08239	Neville Hill T&RSMD	08659	Healey Mills
08254	Gateshead	08660	Cardiff Canton T&RSMD
08285	Doncaster TMD	08667	Neville Hill T&RSMD
08295	Thornaby TMD	08671	Gateshead
08305	Healey Mills	08672	Bescot TMD
08309**F**	Knottingley TMD	08680	Motherwell TMD
08367	Doncaster TMD	08684	Bletchley TMD
08375	Cardiff Canton T&RSMD	08686	Allerton TMD
08385	Hunslet Sidings	08688	Allerton TMD
08390	Landore T&RSMD	08708	Colchester
08407**F**	Stratford TMD	08710	Motherwell TMD
08419	Kingmoor Yard	08712	Motherwell TMD
08420	Doncaster TMD	08719	Bletchley TMD
08427	March TMD	08725	Motherwell TMD
08434	Derby T&RSMD	08727**F**	Motherwell TMD
08439	Immingham TMD	08729	BRML Doncaster
08468	Springs Branch	08741	BRML Doncaster
08473	Leicester	08743	RFS Kilnhurst
08478	Immingham TMD	08744	ABB Crewe
08479	Cardiff Canton T&RSMD	08747	BRML Doncaster
08496	Cambridge T&RSMD	08753	Motherwell TMD
08508	Scunthorpe Yard	08760	BRML Eastleigh
08515	Gateshead	08761**O**	Motherwell TMD
08518	March TMD	08771	Heaton T&RSMD
08532	Allerton TMD	08777	Hull Botanic Gardens
08533	Colchester	08778**D**	Cardiff Canton T&RSMD
08537**FO**	Bescot TMD	08787	ABB Crewe
08539	ABB Crewe	08789	Bletchley TMD
08544	Heaton T&RSMD	08791**F**	Millerhill
08556	Willesden TMD	08794	Neville Hill T&RSMD
08570**M**	Motherwell TMD	08797	Thornaby TMD
08579	Hunslet Sidings	08800**I**	Bristol Bath Road TMD
08584	ABB Crewe	08803**D**	Reading T&RSMD
08589	Cardiff Canton T&RSMD	08804	Cardiff Canton T&RSMD
08591	Ayr TMD	08814	Derby T&RSMD
08608	Gateshead	08821	Laira T&RSMD
08614	Willesden TMD	08822	Cardiff Canton T&RSMD
08618	Gateshead	08831	Eastleigh T&RSMD
08626	Allerton TMD	08836	Cardiff Canton T&RSMD
08631**N**	March TMD	08838	Derby T&RSMD
08634	Stratford TMD	08839	Laira T&RSMD
08638**BS**	Reading T&RSMD	08840	Allerton TMD
08647**G**	BRML Doncaster	08841	ABB Crewe
08652	Cardiff Canton T&RSMD	08848	Cardiff Canton T&RSMD
08654	Cardiff Canton T&RSMD	08850	Reading T&RSMD

08857	ABB Crewe
08858	Allerton TMD
08859	March TMD
08868	March TMD
08870	Doncaster TMD
08885	Doncaster TMD
08889	March TMD
08898	Bescot TMD
08916	Allerton TMD
08917	Allerton TMD
08929	Old Oak Common TMD
08935	Bristol Bath Road TMD
08936	March TMD
08945	Exeter
08949	Bristol Bath Road TMD
20008 **BS**	ABB Crewe
20009	Thornaby TMD
20010 **FR**	Falkland Junction
20011	Derby T&RSMD
20013	Falkland Junction
20019	Toton TMD
20025	Scunthorpe Yard
20028 **BS**	Toton TMD
20029	Falkland Junction
20042	Scunthorpe Yard
20043	Scunthorpe Yard
20058	Toton TMD
20061	Scunthorpe Yard
20068	Immingham TMD
20078	Falkland Junction
20080	BRML Doncaster
20089	Immingham TMD
20099	Springs Branch
20112	Falkland Junction
20119	Toton TMD
20122 **FR**	BRML Glasgow
20124	BRML Glasgow
20140	Toton TMD
20141 **FR**	Falkland Junction
20143	Springs Branch
20144	Thornaby TMD
20148	Toton TMD
20156 **FR**	BRML Glasgow
20160	Bescot Yard
20163 **FR**	Falkland Junction
20170 **FR**	Toton TMD
20172	Toton TMD
20174	Thornaby TMD
20176	Scunthorpe Yard
20181	Bescot Yard
20182	Toton TMD
20185	Falkland Junction
20188	MC Metals, Glasgow
20196	Falkland Junction
20197	Toton TMD
20198	BRML Glasgow
20199	BRML Glasgow
20202	Springs Branch
20210	Toton TMD
20211	BRML Glasgow
20212	BRML Glasgow
20220	Kingmoor Yard
20221	Kingmoor Yard
20223	Kingmoor Yard
25080	Basford Hall Yard
25194	Bescot Yard
25205	Bescot Yard
25206	BRML Doncaster
25211	Bescot Yard
25259	Bescot Yard
26002 **FC**	Inverness T&RSMD
26004 **C**	Inverness T&RSMD
26008 **C**	Inverness T&RSMD
26010	Inverness T&RSMD
26011 **C**	Motherwell TMD
26014	Perth
26015	Inverness T&RSMD
26021	Inverness T&RSMD
26024	Motherwell TMD
26026 **C**	Perth
26027	Perth
26035 **C**	Inverness T&RSMD
26038 **FR**	Inverness T&RSMD
26039	MC Metals, Glasgow
26040 **C**	Perth
26041 **FR**	Inverness T&RSMD
26042	Perth
26043 **C**	Perth
26046	BRML Glasgow
31010	Bescot Yard
31108 **FO**	Scunthorpe Yard
31123	Bescot Yard
31156	Scunthorpe Yard
31162	Immingham TMD
31168	Bescot Yard
31196 **C**	Stratford TMD
31210 **FO**	Scunthorpe Yard
31212	Scunthorpe Yard
31215 **FO**	Immingham TMD
31221	Scunthorpe Yard
31223	Immingham TMD
31240 **FO**	Stratford TMD

▲ Two-tone green liveried Class 47 No. 47833 'Captain Peter Manisty RN' passing Leeds Holbeck with a VSOE Pullman from Appleby – York on 10th April 1993. *Davic C Rodgers*

▼ Central Services liveried Class 47 No. 47972 'The Royal Army Ordnance Corps' is seen leaving Salisbury with the Mobile Track Assesment test train on 22nd April 1993. *Hugh Ballantyne*

Celebrity Class 50s: Nos. D400 & green 50007 'SIR EDWARD ELGAR' pass Pye Bridge on 13th June 1992 with the 'Cavat Charter' railtour.

Ian A. Lyall

▲ Trainload Construction liveried Class 56 No. 56062 on a Wakefield – Cardiff Tidal sidings steel train passes 56081 heading north on a m.g.r. train at Clay Cross on 16th September 1992.　　　　　　　　　　　　　　*Paul Senior*

▼ Trainload Coal Class 58 No. 58013 at Clay Mills near Burton-on-Trent with Barrow Hill – Didcot PS m.g.r. on 14th January 1992.　　　　　*A O Wynn*

ARC owned class 59 No. 59101, now named 'Village of Whatley' passes Great Wishford on 29th January 1992 with the 12.10 Whatley Quarry – Fareham service.

Nic Joynson

▲ Class 60 No. 60064 'Back Tor' in Trainload Petroleum livery passes west-bound through Melton Ross on 29th September 1992.   *Ian A Lyall*

▼ Southern Green Class 73 No. 73003 'Sir Herbert Walker' at Selhurst on 31st March 1993.   *Brian Morrison*

Class 86 No. 86261 in Rail Express Systems livery passing Slindon on 7th September 1992 with the 15.30 Euston – Crewe Postal.

Hugh Ballantyne

A laden Freightliner is hauled through Colchester on 23rd October 1992 by Railfreight Distribution Class 90 No. 90149.

John Augustson

Intercity Class 91 No. 91001 'Swallow' draws into York with the 08.00 Kings Cross – Glasgow Central Pullman service on 30th July 1992.

John Augustson

31243 **FO**	Stratford TMD
31249	Scunthorpe Yard
31264	Thornaby TMD
31283 **O**	Stratford TMD
31286	Bescot Yard
31289	Bescot Yard
31293	Stratford TMD
31299 **FO**	Stratford TMD
31305	Bescot Yard
31320	Stratford TMD
31324 **FC**	Crewe Diesel TMD
31402	Bescot Yard
31404	BRML Doncaster
31428	Basford Hall Yard
31970 **O**	ABB Crewe
33006	BRML Eastleigh
33009 **C**	BRML Eastleigh
33020	Stewarts Lane T&RSMD
33023	Stewarts Lane T&RSMD
33029	Stewarts Lane T&RSMD
33033 **FA**	Stewarts Lane T&RSMD
33038	Stratford TMD
33040	Stewarts Lane T&RSMD
33047 **C**	Eastleigh T&RSMD
33050 **FA**	Stewarts Lane T&RSMD
33058	BRML Eastleigh
33101 **D**	Eastleigh T&RSMD
33102	Eastleigh T&RSMD
33103 **C**	Eastleigh T&RSMD
33108 **C**	Eastleigh T&RSMD
33110	Eastleigh T&RSMD
33113	Stewarts Lane T&RSMD
33114 **N**	Eastleigh T&RSMD
33117	Stewarts Lane T&RSMD
33118 **C**	Eastleigh T&RSMD
33205 **FD**	Stewarts Lane T&RSMD
37008 **FR**	Tinsley TMD
37273 **FP**	Cardiff Canton T&RSMD
37681 **FA**	ABB Crewe
45013	March Whitemoor Yard
45015	Toton TMD
45041	Thornaby TMD
45058	March Whitemoor Yard
45062	March Whitemoor Yard
45076	March Whitemoor Yard
45114	March Whitemoor Yard
45119	March Whitemoor Yard
45121	Derby T&RSMD
45122	March Whitemoor Yard
45127	March Whitemoor Yard
45137	March Whitemoor Yard

45139	March Whitemoor Yard
45142	March Whitemoor Yard
45143	March Whitemoor Yard
46023	Basford Hall Yard
47001	Basford Hall Yard
47002	Doncaster Belmont Yard
47007 **FA**	Doncaster Belmont Yard
47008	Stratford TMD
47010 **FP**	Immingham TMD
47011	ABB Crewe
47015	Basford Hall Yard
47018 **FO**	Doncaster TMD
47054 **FP**	Immingham TMD
47094 **FP**	Scunthorpe Yard
47096	Tinsley TMD
47098	Eastleigh Yard
47099 **FO**	Doncaster Belmont Yard
47100	Doncaster Belmont Yard
47101	Basford Hall Yard
47102	Tinsley TMD
47107 **FO**	Doncaster Belmont Yard
47110	Thornaby TMD
47112 **FO**	Old Oak Common TMD
47115	Scunthorpe Yard
47116	ABB Crewe
47117	Doncaster Belmont Yard
47118 **BR**	Healey Mills
47119 **FP**	Immingham TMD
47120 **BR**	Doncaster Belmont Yard
47123	Doncaster TMD
47143	Doncaster TMD
47159	Thornaby TMD
47191	Springs Branch
47195 **FP**	Tinsley TMD
47198	Cardiff Canton T&RSMD
47199	Kingmoor Yard
47215 **FO**	Eastleigh Yard
47227 **FR**	Tinsley TMD
47233 **FP**	Scunthorpe Yard
47324 **FP**	Immingham TMD
47327 **FO**	Immingham TMD
47373 **FP**	Scunthorpe Yard
47374 **FO**	Immingham TMD
47380 **FP**	Scunthorpe Yard
47381 **FP**	Scunthorpe Yard
47406 **IO**	Scunthorpe Yard
47407 **BR**	Scunthorpe Yard
47411 **BR**	Scunthorpe Yard
47413 **BR**	Scunthorpe Yard
47417	Scunthorpe Yard
47418	Scunthorpe Yard

47421	Crewe Diesel TMD	47472	Old Oak Common TMD
47423	Old Oak Common TMD	47508**M**	Bristol Bath Road TMD
47424**BR**	ABB Crewe	47509**I**	Bristol Bath Road TMD
47425	Old Oak Common TMD	47515**M**	Holbeck
47426**BR**	Old Oak Common TMD	47518**BR**	Immingham TMD
47430**FA**	Old Oak Common TMD	47527**M**	Bristol Bath Road TMD
47431**BR**	Old Oak Common TMD	47533**R**	Old Oak Common TMD
47432**BR**	Gresty Lane	47534**BR**	ABB Crewe
47433**BR**	Crewe Diesel TMD	47538**BR**	ABB Crewe
47434**BR**	Basford Hall Yard	47542	Stratford TMD
47435	Basford Hall Yard	47549**IO**	Crewe Diesel TMD
47436**BR**	Inverness T&RSMD	47585**BR**	Holbeck
47438**BR**	Old Oak Common TMD	47633**BR**	BRML Glasgow
47439**BR**	Crewe Diesel TMD	47643**IO**	Inverness T&RSMD
47440**BR**	Old Oak Common TMD	50029**N**	Laira T&RSMD
47441**BR**	Old Oak Common TMD	50030**N**	Laira T&RSMD
47442**BR**	Crewe Diesel TMD	56002**FC**	Doncaster TMD
47444**BR**	Basford Hall Yard	56017**FC**	Toton TMD
47445**FD**	Doncaster Belmont Yard	56042**F**	Toton TMD
47446**BR**	Old Oak Common TMD	56122**FC**	Toton TMD
47447**BR**	Doncaster Belmont Yard	73004**O**	Stewarts Lane T&RSMD
47448**BR**	Holbeck	73111**IO**	Selhurst TMD
47449**BR**	Stratford TMD	73112**N**	Stewarts Lane T&RSMD
47451**BR**	Doncaster Belmont Yard	82003	Crewe Electric TMD
47452**BR**	Old Oak Common TMD	82005	Crewe Electric TMD
47453**BR**	Old Oak Common TMD	83009	Crewe Electric TMD
47454**BR**	Doncaster Belmont Yard	85013	Crewe Electric TMD
47455**BR**	ABB Crewe	85017	Crewe Electric TMD
47457**BR**	Old Oak Common TMD	85020	Crewe Electric TMD
47458**R**	Crewe Diesel TMD	85028	Crewe Electric TMD
47461**PS**	Basford Hall Yard	85029	Crewe Electric TMD
47465**BR**	Old Oak Common TMD	85101	Crewe Electric TMD
47466**BR**	Holbeck	85107	Crewe Electric TMD
47470**M**	ABB Crewe	97653**O**	Reading T&RSMD

Non-Standard Liveries:

08761 Provincial grey light blue, white and dark blue
20160 BR blue, but with red cab & silver roof
31283 Blue with large numbers
31970 Research light grey, dark grey, white and red
73004 NSE blue
97250 BR carriage blue & grey
97653 Departmental yellow

POOL CODES & ALLOCATIONS

CENTRAL SERVICES

CDJB   Research. BS.

20066   20087   20092 **CS** 20118 **FR** 20132 **FR** 20137 **FR** 20138 **FR**
20165 **FR** 20169 **CS** 47971 **BR** 47972 **CS** 47973 **M** 47975 **C** 47976 **C**

CDJX   Research. Stored.

20090 **FR**

CEJB   Civil Link. BS.

31102 **C** 31105 **C** 31106 **C** 31107 **C** 31110 **C** 31112 **C** 31113 **C**
31125 **C** 31405 **M** 31415   31460   31462 **D** 31467   47300 **C**
47332 **C** 47333 **C** 47341 **C** 47353 **C** 47356 **FO** 47357 **C** 47372 **C**

TRAINLOAD FREIGHT SECTOR

FABI   Construction. IM (based at Buxton).

37677 **FA** 37680 **FA** 60005 **FA** 60015 **FA** 60016 **FA** 60080 **FA** 60082 **FA**
60084 **FA** 60085 **FA** 60095 **FA** 60097 **FA**

FASB   Construction. SL.

56033 **FA** 56035 **FA** 56037 **FA** 56041 **FA** 56051 **FA** 56055 **FA** 56056 **FA**
56057 **FA** 56058 **FA** 56059 **FA** 56065 **FA** 56070 **FA** 56103 **FA** 56105 **FA**
60001 **FA** 60017 **FA** 60018 **FA** 60019 **FA** 60039 **FA** 60040 **FA** 60041 **FA**
60042 **FA** 60043 **FA**

FAXN   Construction. TO (based at Leicester).

60006 **FA** 60009 **FA** 60010 **FA** 60011 **FA** 60012 **FA** 60048 **FA** 60083 **FA**
60094 **FA** 60098 **FA** 60099 **FA** 60100 **FA**

FCBN   Power Station Coal. TO Class 56 & 58 (East Midlands).

56005 **FC** 56006 **FC** 56007 **FC** 56009 **FC** 56010 **FC** 56011 **FR** 56018 **FC**
56021 **FC** 58001 **FC** 58002 **FC** 58003 **FC** 58004 **FC** 58005 **FC** 58006 **FC**
58007 **FC** 58008 **FC** 58009 **FC** 58010 **FC** 58011 **FC** 58012 **FC** 58013 **FC**
58014 **FC** 58015 **FC** 58016 **FC** 58017 **FC** 58018 **FC** 58019 **FC** 58020 **FC**
58021 **FC** 58022 **FC** 58023 **FC** 58024 **FC** 58025 **FC** 58026 **FC** 58027 **FC**
58028 **FC** 58029 **FC** 58030 **FC** 58031 **FC** 58032 **FC** 58033 **FC** 58034 **FC**
58035 **FC** 58036 **FC** 58037 **FC** 58038 **FC** 58041 **FC**

FCCI   Coal. IM Class 47.

47319 **FP**

FCDN   Power Station Coal. TO Class 56 & 58 (Yorkshire).

56023 **FC** 56027 **FC** 56067 **FC** 56068 **FC** 56071 **FC** 56072 **FC** 56074 **FC**
56075 **FC** 56077 **FC** 56078 **FA** 56079 **FC** 56080 **FC** 56081 **FC** 56082 **FC**
56083 **FC** 56084 **FC** 56085 **FC** 56086 **FC** 56088 **FC** 56089 **FC** 56090 **FC**

56091 **FC** 56092 **FC** 56093 **FC** 56095 **FC** 56096 **FC** 56098 **FC** 56099 **FC**
56100 **FC** 56101 **FC** 58039 **FC** 58040 **FC** 58042 **FC** 58043 **FC** 58044 **FC**
58045 **FC** 58046 **FC** 58047 **FC** 58048 **FC** 58049 **FC** 58050 **FC**

FCEN   Power Station Coal. TO Class 56 (North East).

56062 **FA** 56094 **FC** 56102 **FC** 56106 **FC** 56107 **FC** 56108 **FR** 56109 **FC**
56110 **FA** 56111 **FC** 56112 **FC** 56117 **FC** 56118 **FC** 56120 **FC** 56126 **BR**
56130 **FC** 56131 **FC** 56132 **FC** 56133 **FC** 56134 **FC** 56135 **FC**

FCFN   Nuclear Flask Traffic. TO Class 31.

31130 **FC** 31199 **FC** 31200 **FC** 31201 **FC** 31275 **FC** 31302 **FP** 31304 **FC**
31312 **FC** 31319 **FC**

FCHN   Power Station Coal. TO Class 60 (North West).

60032 **FC** 60044 **FM** 60045 **FC** 60046 **FC** 60047 **FC** 60055 **FC** 60056 **FC**
60057 **FC** 60058 **FC** 60060 **FC** 60061 **FC** 60066 **FC**

FCJN   Power Station Coal. TO Class 60 (East Midlands).

60004 **FC** 60059 **FC** 60067 **FC** 60068 **FC** 60069 **FC** 60070 **FC** 60071 **FC**
60072 **FC** 60073 **FC** 60074 **FC** 60075 **FC** 60076 **FC** 60077 **FC** 60078 **FC**
60079 **FC** 60086 **FC** 60087 **FC** 60088 **FC** 60089 **FC**

FCKK   Power Station Coal. CF Classes 37 & 56.

37701 **FC** 37702 **FC** 37703 **FC** 37704 **FC** 37796 **FC** 37797 **FC** 37799 **FC**
37802 **FC** 37887 **FC** 37889 **FC** 37894 **FC** 37895 **FC** 37896 **FC** 37897 **FC**
37898 **FC** 37899 **FC** 56113 **FC** 56114 **FC** 56115 **FC** 56119 **FC**

FCPA   Coal & Petroleum. IM Class 37 & TO Class 56 (Scotland).

37690 **FO** 37692 **FC** 37693 **FC** 37695 **FC** 37696 **FC** 56104 **FC** 56121 **FC**
56123 **FC** 56124 **BR** 56125 **FC** 56127 **FC** 56128 **FC** 56129 **FC**

FCXX   Power Station Coal. Stored.

20016   20055   20057   20059 **FR** 20071   20073   20081
20082   20135   20142   20151   20154   20168   20177
20186   20195   56003 **F** 56004   56008   56012 **FC** 56013 **FC**
56014 **FC** 56015 **FC** 56016 **FC** 56019 **FC** 56020   56022   56024 **FO**
56025 **FC** 56026   56028 **FC** 56029 **FC** 56030 **FC** 56066 **FC**

FIJI   Infrastructure. IM.

37501 **FM** 37513 **FM** 37515 **FM** 37517 **FM** 37519 **FM** 37691 **FO**

FIJW   Infrastructure. IM (weekend work).

37241 **FM** 37502 **FM** 37512 **FM** 37687 **FA**

FMCK   Metals. CF Class 56.

56032 **FM** 56038 **FM** 56040 **FM** 56044 **FM** 56053 **FA** 56054 **FC** 56060 **FA**
56064 **FA** 56073 **FM** 56076 **FC**

FMEK   Metals. CF Class 60.

60029 **FM** 60034 **FM** 60035 **FM** 60036 **FM** 60037 **FM** 60081 **FA** 60093 **FC**
60096 **FA**

FMHK Metals. CF Class 37/7 & 37/9.

37901 FM 37902 FM 37904 FM 37906 FM

FMMK Metals. CF Class 37/9 (reserve).

37903 FM 37905 FM

FMMY Metals. TE Class 60.

60020 FM 60022 FM 60023 FM 60030 FM 60031 FM 60038 FM 60049 FM
60052 FM

FMPY Metals. TE Class 37.

37514 FM 37516 FM

FMTY Metals. TE Class 56.

56034 FA 56043 FA 56045 FA 56050 FA 56061 FM 56063 FA 56069 FM
56087 FM 56097 FM 56116 FC

FMXX Metals. Stored.

20046   20094   20096   20214

FPCI Petroleum. IM Class 37.

37431 M 37508 FM 37511 FM 37518 FM 37694 FC 37706 FP 37707 FP
37708 FP 37711 FM 37712 F 37713 FM 37714 FM 37715 FM 37717 FM
37719 FP 37798 FC 37800 FC 37801 FC 37803 FC 37883 FM 37884 F
37885 FM 37886 FM 37891 FM 37893 FP

FPDI Petroleum. IM Class 60.

60002 FP 60003 FP 60008 FM 60013 FP 60014 FP 60021 FM 60024 FP
60025 FP 60026 FP 60027 FP 60028 FP 60050 FP 60053 FM 60054 FP
60064 FP 60091 FC

FPEK Petroleum. CF.

37521 FP 37668 FP 37697 FC 60033 FP 60051 FP 60062 FP 60063 FP
60065 FP 60092 FP

FPFR Petroleum. IM Class 37 (based at Ripple Lane).

37667 FP 37676 FA 37678 FA 37679 FA 37705 FP 37709 FP 37710 FM
37890 FP 37892 FP

FPTY Petroleum. TE.

37506 FM 37716 FM 37718 FM 60007 FP 60090 FC

FPYI Petroleum. IM Class 37 (restricted use).

37350 FP 37382 FP 37520 FM 37682 FA 37684 FA 37686 FA 37688 FA
37689 FC 37698 FC 37699 FC

FPYX Petroleum. Stored.

37507 FM 37685 FR 37888 FP

FQXB   Railfreight Headquarters. SL Class 56.

56001 **FA** 56039 **FA**

FSCD   Doncaster Shunters.

08418 **F**	08442 **F**	08500 **0**	08512 **F**	08514	08595	08682
08813 **D**	08824 **F**	08877 **D**	08903			

FSCK   Knottingley Shunters.

08499 **F**	08516 **D**	08525 **F**	08583	08605	08662	08706
08707	08776 **D**	08782	08783	08806 **F**	09005 **D**	09014 **D**

FSCN   Toton Shunters.

08441	08449	08492	08511	08597	08607	08623
08723	08773	08829	09104 **D**	09201 **D**		

FSNH   Heaton Shunters.

08577	08578 **R**	08587	08590 **BS**	08701 **RX**	08802	08886
08888 **R**	08931					

FSNI   Immingham Shunters.

08388 **F**	08401 **D**	08405 **D**	08445	08466 **F0**	08632	08665

FSNL   Neville Hill Shunters.

08389	08575 **BS**	08581	08588 **BS**	08661	08745 **BS**	08908
08950 **I**						

FSNT   Tinsley Shunters.

08509 **F**	08510	08691 **G**	08879	08880	08919	09008 **D**
09013 **D**	09106 **D**					

FSNY   Thornaby Shunters.

08411	08506	08582 **D**	08867 **0**	08906	09103 **D**	09204 **D**

FSSA   Ayr Shunters.

08561	08586 **F**	08675 **F**

FSSB   Aberdeen Shunters.

08793 **0**	08855	08882

FSSI   Inverness Shunters.

08754	08762

FSSM   Motherwell Shunters.

08565	08568	08571	08622	08630	08693	08718
08720 **D**	08730 **0**	08731	08733	08735	08738 **D**	08755
08853	08881 **D**	08883 **0**	08922 **D**	08938 **0**	08952	09202 **D**

FSWK   Cardiff Canton Shunters.

08481	08493	08664	08770 **D**	08786	08795 **D**	08818
08830	08845 **D**	08895	08932	08942	09001	09015 **D**

09105 **D** 09203 **D**

FSWL   Landore Shunters.

08646 **F** 08756 **D** 08780   08798   08896   08993   08994 **FR**
08995 **FC**

INTERCITY SECTOR

IANA   Anglia Services Locos.

86215 **M** 86217 **I** 86218 **I** 86220 **I** 86221 **M** 86223 **I** 86230 **M**
86232 **I** 86235 **I** 86237 **I** 86238 **I** 86246 **I** 86249 **M** 86250 **I**

IBRA   Bristol Class 47/4. Special Use.

47809 **I** 47819 **I** 47820 **I** 47821 **I** 47823 **I** 47833 **G** 47834 **I**
47835 **I**

IBRB   Bristol Class 47/4. General Hire.

47840 **I** 47843 **I** 47851 **I**

ICCA   Cross Country Class 86.

86205 **I** 86206 **M** 86212 **M** 86214 **I** 86216 **I** 86222 **I** 86226 **M**
86227 **M** 86228 **I** 86229 **I** 86233 **I** 86234 **I** 86244 **I** 86247 **I**
86252 **I0** 86255 **I** 86259 **I** 86260 **I**

ICCP   Cross Country Class 43. LA & PM.

43086 **I** 43087 **I** 43088 **I** 43089 **I** 43101 **I** 43102 **I** 43103 **I**
43121 **I** 43122 **I** 43124 **I** 43130 **I** 43132 **I** 43138 **I** 43153 **I**
43154 **I** 43155 **I** 43156 **I** 43157 **I** 43158 **I** 43159 **I** 43160 **I**
43161 **I** 43162 **I** 43170 **I** 43180 **I** 43193 **I** 43194 **I** 43195 **I**
43196 **I** 43197 **I** 43198 **I**

ICCS   Cross Country Class 43. EC.

43013 **I** 43014 **I** 43062 **I** 43063 **I** 43065 **I** 43067 **I** 43068 **I**
43069 **I** 43070 **I** 43071 **I** 43078 **I** 43079 **I** 43080 **I** 43084 **I**
43090 **I** 43091 **I** 43092 **I** 43093 **I** 43094 **I** 43097 **I** 43098 **I**
43099 **I** 43100 **I** 43123 **I**

IECA   ECML Class 91.

91001 **I** 91002 **I** 91003 **I** 91004 **I** 91005 **I** 91006 **I** 91007 **I**
91008 **I** 91009 **I** 91010 **I** 91011 **I** 91012 **I** 91013 **I** 91014 **I**
91015 **I** 91016 **I** 91017 **I** 91018 **I** 91019 **I** 91020 **I** 91021 **I**
91022 **I** 91023 **I** 91024 **I** 91025 **I** 91026 **I** 91027 **I** 91028 **I**
91029 **I** 91030 **I** 91031 **I**

IECP   ECML Class 43.

43038 **I** 43039 **I** 43095 **I** 43096 **I** 43104 **I** 43105 **I** 43106 **I**
43107 **I** 43108 **I** 43109 **I** 43110 **I** 43111 **I** 43112 **I** 43113 **I**
43114 **I** 43115 **I** 43116 **I** 43117 **I** 43118 **I** 43119 **I** 43120 **I**

IEJI   Infrastructure. ECML. IM.

31531 **C** 31541 **C** 31544 **C** 31549 **C** 31552 **C** 31553 **C** 31556 **C**

31558 **C** 37003 **C** 37058 **C** 37095 **C** 37104 **C** 47331 **C** 47520 **M** 47671 **BR** 47673 **I0** 47675 **M** 47676 **I**

IEJW   Infrastructure. ECML. IM. (weekend work).

31149 **FR** 31184 **F0** 31205 **FR** 31276 **FC** 31294 **FA** 31547 **C** 37271 **FD** 47336 **FP** 47550 **M**

IGJA   Infrastructure. GWML BR.

37031 **FD** 37037 **FM** 37040 **FM** 37042 **FM** 37048 **FM** 37065 **FD** 37072 **D** 37074 **FD** 37077 **FM** 37101 **FD** 37109 **FM** 37137 **FM** 37138 **FM** 37203 **FM** 37213 **FC** 37219   37222 **FC** 37223 **FC** 37227 **FM** 37229 **FC**

IGJK   Infrastructure. GWML. CF.

37010 **C** 37012 **C** 37035 **C** 37038 **C** 37046 **C** 37054 **C** 37092 **C** 37097 **C** 37098 **C** 37174 **C** 37264 **C** 37372 **C** 97654 **0** 97806 **0**

IGJO   Infrastructure. GWML. OC.

47315 **C** 47366 **F0**

IGJW   Infrastructure. GWML. OC. (weekend work).

47004 **FA** 47016 **F0** 47019 **F0** 47105   47108   47121   47358 **F0** 47484 **G**

IHFB   M&EE. Overhead Line Maintenance. BS.

31271 **FA** 31403   31407 **M** 31435 **C** 31459   31461 **D** 31466 **C**

IHRB   M&EE. Fleet Maintenance.

31417 **D** 31420 **M** 31422 **M** 31423 **M** 31434   31457 **D**

IISA   Inverness Class 37.

37078 **FM** 37080 **FP** 37113 **FD** 37133 **C** 37152 **I** 37170 **C** 37175 **C** 37214 **FA** 37221 **I** 37250 **FM** 37251 **I** 37262 **D** 37505 **FP** 37510 **I** 37683 **F**

IISW   ECML Class 37 (weekend work).

37066 **C** 37071 **C** 37100 **FM** 37239 **FC**

ILRA   Bristol Class 47/4. Extended Range Locos.

47805 **I** 47806 **I** 47807 **I** 47810 **I** 47811 **I** 47812 **I** 47813 **I** 47814 **I** 47815 **I** 47816 **I** 47817 **I** 47818 **M** 47822 **I** 47825 **M** 47826 **I** 47827 **I** 47828 **I** 47829 **M** 47830 **I** 47831 **M** 47832 **M** 47839 **I** 47841 **I** 47844 **I** 47845 **I** 47846 **I** 47847 **I** 47848 **I** 47849 **M** 47850 **I** 47853 **M**

IMJB   Infrastructure. Midland/Cross Country. BS.

31116 **C** 31119 **C** 31126 **C**

IMJC   Infrastructure. Midland/Cross Country. BR.

47348 **F0** 47368 **FP** 47483 **M** 47555 **I0** 47674 **BR** 47677 **I** 47802 **I** 47803 **0** 47804 **I** 47824 **M**

IMJW   Infrastructure. Midland/Cross Country. BS. (weekend work).

31134 **C**	31145 **C**	31171 **FO**	31209 **FA**	31234 **FO**	31248 **FO** 31252 **FO**
31411 **D**	31413 **O**	31418	31427		

IMLP   Midland Line Class 43.

43043 **I**	43044 **I**	43045 **I**	43046 **I**	43047 **I**	43048 **I** 43049 **I**
43050 **I**	43051 **I**	43052 **I**	43053 **I**	43054 **I**	43055 **I** 43056 **I**
43057 **I**	43058 **I**	43059 **I**	43060 **I**	43061 **I**	43064 **I** 43066 **I**
43072 **I**	43073 **I**	43074 **I**	43075 **I**	43076 **I**	43077 **I** 43081 **I**
43082 **I**	43083 **I**	43085 **I**			

IVGA   Gatwick Express Services Class 73.

73201 **I**	73202 **I**	73203 **I**	73204 **I**	73205 **M**	73206 **I** 73207 **I**
73208 **I**	73209 **I**	73210 **I**	73211 **I**	73212 **I**	73235 **I**

IWCA   WCML Class 87 & 90.

87010 **I**	87011 **M**	87012 **M**	87013 **I**	87014 **I**	87015 **I** 87016 **I**
87017 **IO**	87018 **M**	87019 **IO**	87020 **IO**	87021 **IO**	87022 **M** 87023 **IO**
87024 **IO**	87025 **IO**	87026 **IO**	87027 **IO**	87028 **M**	87029 **IO** 87030 **IO**
87031 **M**	87032 **IO**	87033 **M**	87034 **IO**	87035 **M**	90001 **I** 90002 **I**
90003 **I**	90004 **I**	90005 **I**	90006 **I**	90007 **I**	90008 **I** 90009 **I**
90010 **I**	90011 **I**	90012 **I**	90013 **I**	90014 **I**	90015 **I**

IWCP   WCML Class 43.

43042 **I**	43141 **I**	43142 **I**	43144 **I**	43145 **I**	43146 **I** 43147 **I**

IWJB   Infrastructure. WCML. BS.

31512 **C**	31514 **C**	31516 **C**	31519 **C**	31524 **C**	31526 **C** 31530 **C**
31533 **C**	31537 **C**	31545 **C**	31546 **C**	31548 **C**	31551 **C** 31554 **C**

IWJC   Infrastructure. WCML. CD Class 31.

31142 **C**	31144 **C**	31154 **C**	31159 **C**	31163 **C**	31203 **C** 31206 **C**
31232 **C**	31235 **C**				

IWJD   Infrastructure. WCML. CD Class 47.

47318 **FO**	47329 **C**	47334 **C**	47340 **C**	47473 **BR**	47478 47525 **IO**

IWPA   Euston – West Midlands Services Class 86.

86101 **M**	86102 **IO**	86103 **I**	86204 **I**	86207 **I**	86208 **I** 86209 **M**
86210 **I**	86213 **I**	86219 **I**	86224 **I**	86225 **I**	86231 **I** 86236 **I**
86240 **I**	86242 **M**	86245 **I**	86248 **I**	86251 **M**	86253 **I** 86256 **M**
86257 **I**	86258 **I**				

IWRP   GWML Class 43.

43002 **I**	43003 **I**	43004 **I**	43005 **I**	43006 **I**	43007 **I** 43008 **I**
43009 **I**	43010 **I**	43011 **I**	43012 **I**	43015 **I**	43016 **I** 43017 **I**
43018 **I**	43019 **I**	43020 **I**	43021 **I**	43022 **I**	43023 **I** 43024 **I**
43025 **I**	43026 **I**	43027 **I**	43028 **I**	43029 **I**	43030 **I** 43031 **I**
43032 **I**	43033 **I**	43034 **I**	43035 **I**	43036 **I**	43037 **I** 43040 **I**
43041 **I**	43125 **I**	43126 **I**	43127 **I**	43128 **I**	43129 **I** 43131 **I**

43133 I   43134 I   43135 I   43136 I   43137 I   43139 I   43140 I
43143 I   43148 I   43149 I   43150 I   43151 I   43152 I   43163 I
43164 I   43165 I   43166 I   43167 I   43168 I   43169 I   43171 I
43172 I   43173 I   43174 I   43175 I   43176 I   43177 I   43178 I
43179 I   43181 I   43182 I   43183 I   43184 I   43185 I   43186 I
43187 I   43188 I   43189 I   43190 I   43191 I   43192 I

IWSA   WCML CLass 87. (100 mph maximum).

87001 I   87002 I   87003 I   87004 I   87005 I   87006 I0 87007 I
87008 I   87009 I

IXXS   Stored.

31450

RAILFREIGHT DISTRIBUTION SECTOR

MDAT   Tinsley Class 47.

47052 FD 47147 FD 47187 FD 47207 FD 47238 FD 47279 FD 47288 FD
47289 FD 47296 FD 47301 FR 47302 FR 47305 FP 47339 FD 47347 FM
47359 FD 47367 FR 47376   47377 FD

MDCT   Tinsley Class 47 (based at Saltley).

47033 FD 47051 FD 47219 FD 47222 FD 47236 FD 47237 FD 47280 FD
47285 FD 47310 FD 47313 FD 47316 FD 47323 FD 47326 FD 47362 FD

MDDT   Tinsley Class 47 (extended range).

47049 FD 47053 FD 47085 F 47114 FA 47125 FD 47144 FD 47150 FD
47152 FD 47156 FD 47186 FD 47188 FD 47194 FD 47200 FD 47201 FD
47204 FD 47205 FD 47209 FD 47210 FD 47211 FD 47213 F 47217 FD
47218 FD 47226 FD 47228 FD 47229 FD 47234 FD 47241 FD 47245 FD
47258 FD 47281 FD 47284 FD 47286 F 47287 FD 47290 FD 47291 FD
47292 FD 47293 FD 47297 FD 47298 FD 47299 FD 47303 F 47304 FD
47307 FD 47309 FD 47312 FD 47314 FD 47328 FD 47330 FD 47335 FD
47338 FD 47344 F 47351 FD 47355 FD 47360 FD 47361 FD 47363 F
47365 FD 47375 FD 47378 FD

MDIB   Dover Train Ferry Class 33/2.

33204 FD 33206 FD 33207 FA 33211 FD

MDLC   Crewe Class 90/0.

90022 FD 90023 FD 90024 FD 90025 FD

MDMC   Crewe Class 90/1.

90126 FD 90127 FD 90128 0 90129 0 90130 0 90131 M 90132 M
90133 M 90134 M 90135 M 90136 0 90137 FD 90138 FD 90139 FD
90140 FD 90141 FD 90142 FD 90143 FD 90144 FD 90145 FD 90146 FD
90147 FD 90148 FD 90149 FD 90150 FD

MDNC   Crewe Class 86/6 and 87/1 Locos.

86602 **FD** 86603 **FD** 86604 **FD** 86606 **FD** 86607 **FD** 86608 **FD** 86609 **FD**
86610 **FD** 86612 **FD** 86613 **FD** 86618 **FD** 86620 **FD** 86621 **FD** 86622 **FD**
86623 **FD** 86627 **FD** 86632 **FD** 86633 **FD** 86634 **FD** 86635 **FD** 86636 **FD**
86637 **FD** 86638 **FD** 86639 **FD** 87101 **FD**

MDRL   Laira Refurbished Class 37 (based at St. Blazey).

37411 **FD** 37412 **FD** 37413 **FD** 37416 **M** 37669 **FD** 37670 **FD** 37671 **FD**
37672 **FD** 37673 **FD** 37674 **FD** 37675 **FD**

MDRM   Motherwell Refurbished Class 37.

37401 **M** 37403 **FD** 37406 **M** 37409 **M** 37410 **M** 37423 **M** 37424 **M**
37430 **M**

MDRT   Tinsley Refurbished Class 37.

37358 **F** 37359 **FP** 37378 **FD** 37381 **FM** 37405 **M** 37415 **M** 37417 **M**
37419 **M** 37420 **M** 37426 **M**

MDSR   Tinsley Reserve Class 37.

37009 **FD** 37013 **F** 37045 **F** 37116 **BR** 37235 **F** 37278 **FC** 37280 **FP**
37373 **FR**

MDTT   Tinsley Unrefurbished Class 37 (extended range).

37015 **FD** 37019 **FD** 37026 **FD** 37053 **FD** 37068 **FD** 37073 **FD** 37075 **F**
37079 **FD** 37107 **FD** 37108 **F** 37110 **FD** 37131 **FD** 37154 **FD** 37178 **FD**
37218 **FD** 37225 **FD** 37238 **FD** 37261 **FD** 37298 **FD**

MDWT   Tinsley Classes 37 & 47 (restricted use).

47079 **FD** 47142 **FR** 47145   47146   47157 **F** 47193 **FP** 47196 **FP**
47197 **FP** 47206 **FD** 47212 **FP** 47221 **FP** 47223 **FP** 47224 **FP** 47231 **FD**
47249 **FR** 47256 **FD** 47270   47276 **FP** 47277 **FP** 47278 **FP** 47283 **FD**
47294 **FP** 47308 **F** 47317   47321 **F** 47322 **FR** 47337 **FD** 47345 **FR**
47350 **FO** 47352 **C** 47354 **FD** 47369 **FP** 47370 **FO** 47371 **FO** 47379 **FP**

MDYX   Stored.

37029 **FD** 37032 **FR** 37057 **BR** 37070 **FD** 37209 **BR** 37248 **FM** 37252 **FD**
47050 **FD** 47060 **FD** 47063 **FA** 47095 **FD** 47190 **FP** 47214 **FD** 47220 **FO**
47225 **FD** 47295 **FD** 47306 **FD** 47320 **FD** 47325 **FO** 47349 **FD**

MSCH   Rfd Central Hire Pool. Shunters.

08413 **D** 08417 **D** 08472   08498   08517   08562   08603
08670   08700   08705   08713   08811   08823   08866
08878

MSNA   Allerton Shunters.

08397 **F** 08402 **D** 08415   08482 **D** 08485   08489 **F** 08521
08569   08613   08615   08694   08703   08799   08809
08815   08817 **BS** 08856   08872 **D** 08884   08894   08900 **D**
08902   08913 **D** 08918 **D** 08925   08939   08951 **D**

MSNB   Bescot Shunters.

| 08428 | 08448 | 08535 **D** | 08543 **D** | 08601 **0** | 08610 | 08616 |
| 08734 | 08746 **D** | 08751 | 08765 **D** | 08805 **F0** | 08893 **D** | 08901 |
| 08920 **F** |

MSNC   Crewe Shunters.

| 08585 | 08599 | 08633 **RX** | 08635 | 08692 | 08695 | 08699 |
| 08702 | 08737 **F** | 08739 | 08742 | 08784 | 08907 **0** | 08921 |
| 09102 **D** |

MSNE   Derby Etches Park Shunters.

| 08536 | 08604 **G** | 08697 | 08788 | 08842 | 08899 |

MSNL   Longsight Shunters.

| 08611 | 08619 | 08624 | 08666 | 08673 **I0** | 08676 | 08721 **0** |
| 08790 | 08891 | 08915 **F** |

MSNU   Carlisle Upperby Shunters.

| 08447 | 08534 **D** | 08690 | 08768 | 08826 | 08827 | 08844 |
| 08910 | 08911 **D** | 08912 |

MSSA   Bristol Bath Road Shunters.

| 08410 **D** | 08483 **D** | 08643 **D** | 08668 | 08897 **D** |

MSSB   Bletchley Shunters.

| 08484 **F** | 08519 **BS** | 08567 | 08625 | 08628 | 08629 | 08683 |
| 08807 | 08914 | 08927 |

MSSC   Cambridge Shunters.

| 08594 | 08685 | 08711 | 08714 | 08757 **D** | 08865 |

MSSL   Laira Shunters.

| 08576 | 08641 **D** | 08644 **M** | 08645 **D** | 08663 **D** | 08792 | 08801 |
| 08819 **D** | 08849 | 08937 **D** | 08941 | 08953 **D** | 08954 **F** | 08955 |

MSSM   March Shunters.

| 08495 | 08528 **D** | 08529 | 08538 **D** | 08540 **D** | 08580 |

MSSN   Norwich Shunters.

| 08810 | 08869 **G** | 08928 **FR** |

MSSO   Old Oak Common Shunters.

| 08460 **F** | 08480 | 08651 **D** | 08653 | 08825 | 08837 **D** | 08904 |
| 08944 **D** | 08947 | 08948 |

MSSR   Reading Shunters.

| 08507 | 08523 | 08905 | 08924 **D** | 08946 **D** | 09101 **D** |

MSSS   Stratford Shunters.

08393 **D**	08414	08526	08527 **D**	08530 **D**	08531 **F**	08541 **D**
08542 **F**	08573	08593	08627	08655 **F**	08689	08698
08709	08715	08724	08740 **F**	08748	08750	08752 **C**
08758	08767	08772 **G**	08775	08828	08834 **F**	08873 **M**
08909	08923 **F**	08956	08957	08958		

MSSW   Willesden Shunters.

08451	08454	08609	08617	08648 **D**	08677	08696 **D**
08887	08890 **D**	08926	08934			

NETWORK SOUTH-EAST SECTOR

NKFE   Infrastructure. South electrification. EH.

37194 **FD** 37220 **FP** 37245 **C** 37293 **FM** 37380 **FC**

NKFH   Infrastructure. North electrification. he.

97703	97704	97705	97706	97707 **N**	97708 **N** 97709
97710					

NKJD   Infrastructure. South. EH & RY Shunters.

03079   08600 **D** 08847   08892 **D** 08933 **0** 08940

NKJE   Infrastructure. South. EH.

33008 **G** 33019 **C** 33025 **C** 33030 **C** 33035 **N** 33046 **C** 33051 **C**
33116 **D** 37198 **C** 37274 **C** 37375 **C** 37377 **C**

NKJH   Infrastructure. South. AF & SU Shunters.

08642 **0**	08649 **D**	08854	09003	09004	09006	09007
09009 **D**	09010 **D**	09011 **D**	09012 **D**	09016 **D**	09018	09019 **D**
09020	09021	09022	09023	09024 **D**	09025	09026 **D**

NKJL   Infrastructure. South. SL.

73101 **0** 73103 **I0** 73104 **I0** 73105 **C** 73106 **D** 73107 **C** 73108 **C**
73110 **C** 73117 **I0** 73118 **C** 73119 **C** 73129 **N** 73130 **C** 73133 **N**
73136 **N** 73138 **C**

NKJM   Infrastructure. EH. Meldon Quarry duties.

33057 **C** 33064 **FA** 33109 **D** 33201 **C** 33202 **C** 33208 **C** 56031 **C**
56036 **C** 56046 **C** 56047 **FC** 56048 **FR** 56049 **C** 56052 **FA**

NKJR   Infrastructure. South (restricted use).

33002 **C** 33012   33021 **FA** 33026 **C** 33042 **FA** 33048   33052
33053 **FA** 33063 **FA** 33065 **C** 73114 **I0** 73126 **N** 73128 **C** 73131 **C**
73132 **I0** 73134 **I0** 73139 **I0** 73140 **I0** 73141 **I0**

NKJS   Infrastructure. North. SF.

31135 **C** 31224 **C** 31250 **C** 31290 **C** 37023 **C** 37047 **FD** 37055 **FD**
37140 **C** 37242 **FD** 37244 **FD** 37370 **C** 37371 **C** 37376 **FC** 37379 **C**
47364 **C**

NKJW   Infrastructure. North (weekend work).

31165 **G** 31180 **FR** 31181 **C** 31191 **C** 31268 **C**

NTWH   West of England/North Downs Services. EH Class 47.

47701 **N** 47702 **N** 47703 **R** 47705 **N** 47715 **N** 47716 **N** 47717 **R**

NWXA   West of England/North Downs Services. LA Class 50.

50007 **G** 50033 **N** 50050

NWXB   West of England/North Downs Services. BM Class 73.

73109 **N**

NXXA   General.

73003 **G**

NXXB   Awaiting Transfer. Class 47.

47526 **BR** 47579 **N** 47711 **N**

RAIL EXPRESS SYSTEMS SECTOR

PXLA   Crewe Class 90.

90016 **RX** 90017 **RX** 90018 **RX** 90019 **RX** 90020 **RX** 90021 **FD**

PXLB   Crewe Class 47. (extended range).

47490 **RX** 47491 **RX** 47500 **RX** 47503 **RX** 47517 **RX** 47531 **RX** 47537 **RX**
47541 **RX** 47551 **RX** 47559 **RX** 47562 **RX** 47573 **RX** 47578 **RX** 47581 **RX**
47606 **RX** 47612 **RX** 47618 **RX** 47630 **RX** 47631 **RX** 47636 **RX** 47642 **RX**
47704 **RX** 47706 **PS** 47707 **N** 47708 **N** 47709 **N** 47710 **N** 47712 **R**
47714 **N** 47808 **I**

PXLC   Crewe Class 47.

47443 **BR** 47462 **R** 47463   47467 **BR** 47471 **IO** 47474 **R** 47475 **RX**
47476 **R** 47481 **BR** 47482 **BR** 47485 **BR** 47488 **BR** 47489 **R** 47492 **IO**
47501 **BR** 47513 **BR** 47519 **BR** 47521 **N** 47522 **R** 47523 **M** 47524 **M**
47528 **M** 47530 **RX** 47532 **RX** 47535 **R** 47536 **BR** 47539 **RX** 47543 **R**
47547 **N** 47557 **M** 47558 **M** 47565 **M** 47566 **M** 47567 **M** 47568 **RX**
47569 **R** 47572 **R** 47574 **R** 47575 **R** 47576 **RX** 47580 **BR** 47582 **R**
47583 **N** 47584 **M** 47587 **N** 47588 **RX** 47592 **BR** 47594 **RX** 47596 **N**
47597 **RX** 47598 **RX** 47599 **RX** 47600 **RX** 47603 **BR** 47605 **RX** 47615 **RX**
47624 **M** 47625 **RX** 47626 **M** 47627 **RX** 47628 **RX** 47634 **R** 47635 **RX**
47640 **R**

PXLD   Parcels Reserve and Stored Locos.

47564 **BR** 47641 **BR** 47644 **BR**

PXLE   Crewe Class 86.

86239 **R** 86241 **R** 86243 **IO** 86254 **RX** 86261 **RX** 86401 **RX** 86405 **FD**
86411 **FD** 86414 **FD** 86415 **FD** 86416 **RX** 86417 **RX** 86419 **R** 86424 **R**
86425 **R** 86426 **RX** 86428 **FD** 86430 **RX** 86431 **FD**

REGIONAL RAILWAYS SECTOR

RAIL Scotrail. IS Class 97/2.

97251 **M** 97252 **M**

RAJE Infrastructure. Scotrail. IS Class 26.

26001 **G** 26003 **C** 26005 **C** 26007 **G**

RAJP Infrastructure. Scotrail. IS Class 37/4.

37427 **FA** 37428 **FP**

RAJV Infrastructure. Scotrail. IS Class 37.

37004 **FM** 37025 **C** 37043 **C** 37051 **FM** 37069 **C** 37087 **C** 37088 **D**
37099 **FM** 37106 **C** 37111 **FM** 37153 **C** 37156 **C** 37165 **C** 37167 **FC**
37184 **C** 37188 **FP** 37196 **C** 37201 **FM** 37211 **FA** 37212 **FC** 37232 **C**
37240 **C** 37255 **FM** 37275 **FM** 37294 **C** 37351 **C** 37402 **M** 37404 **M**

RBJI Infrastructure. North East. IM.

37049 **C** 37083 **C** 37139 **FC** 37144 **FA**

RBJW Infrastructure. North East. IM (weekend work).

31230 **FO** 31247 **FR** 31563 **C** 37059 **FD** 37063 **FD** 37128 **BR** 37202 **FM**
37217   37272 **FD** 37285 **F** 47346 **C**

RCJC Infrastructure. North West. CD Class 31.

31188 **C** 31207 **C** 31229 **C** 31233 **C** 31238 **C** 31242 **C** 31255 **C**
31272 **C** 31285 **C** 31306 **C**

RCKC Infrastructure. North West. CD Class 31/4.

31408   31410 **RR** 31421 **RR** 31432   31438   31439 **RR** 31442
31455 **RR** 31465 **RR**

RCLC Infrastructure. North West. CD Class 47.

37503 **FM** 37504 **FM** 37509 **FM**

RCMC Infrastructure. North West. CD Class 37/4.

37407 **M** 37408 **BR** 37414 **RR** 37418 **FP** 37421 **FP** 37422 **RR** 37425 **FA**
37429 **RR**

RCRB Infrastructure. North West. BD.

73001   73002 **BR** 73005 **0** 73006 **BR** 97701 **0** 97702 **0**

RCWC Infrastructure. North West. CD Class 31 (weekend work).

31160 **F** 31190 **C** 31217 **FC** 31263 **C** 31270 **FC** 31282 **FR** 31296 **FA**
31301 **FR** 31327 **FR**

RDDJ Infrastructure. Central. BS (RETB fitted).

31146 **C** 31147 **C** 31158 **C** 31166 **C**

RDJB   Infrastructure. Central. BS Class 31.

31155 **C** 31174 **C** 31178 **C** 31185 **C** 31237 **C** 31273 **C** 31308 **C**
31468 **C**

RDJM   Infrastructure. Central. SF (based at March).

31186 **C** 31219 **C**

RDJS   Infrastructure. Central. SF.

31187 **C** 37216 **G**

RDJW   Infrastructure. Central. BS Class 31 (weekend work).

31128 **FO** 31132 **FO** 31164 **FO** 31317 **FO** 31569 **C**

RDKB   Infrastructure. Central. BS Class 37.

37114 **C** 37162 **D** 37185 **C**

REJK   Infrastructure. South Wales & West. CF.

37141 **C** 37142 **C** 37146 **C** 37158 **C** 37191 **C** 37197 **C** 37207 **C**
37230 **C** 37254 **C** 37258 **C** 37263 **C** 97651 **O**

RFJX   Infrastructure. Stored.

26006 **FC** 26025 **C** 26032 **FR** 26036 **C** 26037 **FR** 37190 **FM** 37215 **FP**

BR TELECOMS LOCOS

TAKB   BR Telecoms. BS.

20007   20032   20075   20104 **FR** 20128   20131   20187

TAKX   BR Telecoms. Stored.

20072   20106   20117   20121   20190   20215 **FR**

PRIVATELY-OWNED LOCOS

XYPA   ARC Class 59/1.

59101 **O** 59102 **O** 59103 **O** 59104 **O**

XYPD   Hunslet-Barclay Class 20/9.

20901 **O** 20902 **O** 20903 **O** 20904 **O** 20905 **O** 20906 **O**

XYPO   Foster-Yeoman Class 59/0.

59001 **O** 59002 **O** 59003 **O** 59004 **O** 59005 **O**